JAZZMEN

'Then entertain conjecture of a time. . .'

Compiled and edited by

Laurie Dex

First Published 1991

By: Beck Books

29 St Mary' Mount,

Station Road,

Cottingham

Hull HU16 4LQ

A Limited Edition of

Six Hundred copies

of which this is No.

Printed in England by
The Print Industry, Hull

ISBN   0 9514750 2 9 Hull Jazz and Jazzmen. (pbk)

Dedicated to the Memory of:
Tony Grunhill
Al Jenner
Brian 'Slow Drag' Kirby

Bob Wallis
and all other Hull Jazzmen
past and present

Preface, Foreword, Apologia

Really I ought to have known better than to attempt to compile this slim volume. It seemed to be a good idea at the time, the time probably being late on a Friday evening just after I had had my weekly fix of jazz at the King Billy.

To anyone who has never tried to put together something about local history, local sub-culture, call it what you will, I can only ask for comparison with trying to do a 1,000 piece jigsaw. To start with you haven't got a level space big enough, there are certain complications when you realise that the whole thing is at least 50 pieces short, the picture on the lid of the box, missing.

The time comes when you are quite prepared to jack the whole thing in. And who could blame you but yourself.

However, in this case I had a pile of voluntary contributions on my hands from people I know and whose playing I have enjoyed. Hard luck, Dex. Stop moaning and get on with it. So I did, and here it is, warts and all. May I also add, E.& O.E.

Contents

Bill and Joyce Cater

Bill   For me it was when I was about 17 or 18, that would be 1952/3 and a man I worked with persuaded me to go to a Club that had opened at the East Park Ballroom called The Rhythm Club. I can't remember too much of the line up but I am sure Ken Ford and Eric Dobson played two banjos in the Band, Tony Grunhill was on drums and Al Jenner on trumpet. The Club later moved to Wright Street but I didn't play there. When I was about 19 I bought a trumpet, funnily enough I was a fan of Eddie Calvert at the time and we formed a band in Beverley with Brian Vincent and Bob Penwarn. They needed a trombone player, and the only other person interested in playing in the band was a trumpeter named Dennis. We tossed up for it, I lost, so Dennis played the trumpet and I had to go and buy a trombone and I've been playing the thing ever since! We played up there at Cross Keys for a couple of months and then got the sack. The band broke up, it was fairly useless anyway and Brian Vincent and I started going through to Hull to the various Jazz venues around.

Joyce   Up to then I had a very sheltered upbringing and my personal life was involved with the Church. When I was 17, David Turner who was a trombone player came and gave a talk for the Youth Club and he introduced me to Humphrey Littleton and Chris Barber, who I thought were marvellous. This was just before I left Hull to go to College, in Sheffield. Here I was open to much wider influences, a much broader spectrum. It was in Sheffield that I became a real enthusiast. I listened to both traditional and modern jazz at the clubs,

1

of which there were many. The jazz clubs in those days consisted of a hall, low lights, orange boxes to sit on, drinks and cigarette smoke. I began trying to play jazz piano, but very badly. During my holidays, which I spent in London, I visited the Ken Colyer Club and 100 Oxford Street which were packed full and very hot. When I returned to Hull during other holidays, I used to cycle to University and to the Cottingham Rhythm Club, especially when Chez Chesterman was playing. I didn't know many people at this time and used to go out on my own, curl up in an armchair at the University and just get lost in the music. I returned to Hull College in 1959 and found my way to the Abercrombie pub in Campbell Street and a trombone player called Bill. Bill and I don't quite know how to go on from here because I've kept a detailed diary from which I've made lists of the gigs we played and a lot of musicians. I think the best thing we can do is to present Laurie with this book and Bill and I will just make comments on each year.

Two years of Jazz events as recorded by Joyce Cater 1960-1961

1960

Jazz recitals continued at Gough and Davy's during the winter. Records. Friday the Unity Band played at the Blue Bell.

Sunday Club at the University.

The Red Cellar Jazz Club in Kingston Square open on Tuesday nights.

April 8th.	Kenny Ball at Windsor Hall.
April 10th.	Chris Barber and Sister Rosetta Thorpe at the City Hall.
April 29th.	Sandy Brown Band at the Windsor Hall.
May 12th.	Mike Gordon and Glenn Gibb sat in at the Abercrombie.
May 23rd.	2-19 split up.
May 30th	2-19 reformed as the Burgundy Band

2

June 10th.	Geoff Woodhouse band plus the Unity Band at Windsor Hall.
June 11th.	Riverboat Shuffle, five bands including Alex Welsh.
June 21st.	Another Riverboat Shuffle.
July 3rd.	Band in East Park. The Burgundy. Bill, John H. Ted Blackshaw, Tony Grunhill, Brian Vincent, Joyce.
July 13th.	Burgundy started at Blue Bell.
July 15th.	Burgundy at the Windsor Hall, paid 10/- each! July 27th & 28th. Ches Chesterman played trumpet with the Band (Blue Bell)
August 8th.	Third Riverboat Shuffle this year, Nat Gonella, 25/- each.
August 28th.	Chris Barber, Spa, Brid.
September 9th.	Mick Mulligan, Windsor Hall.
September 23rd.	Mike Peters Jazz Band at the Windsor.
September 30th.	Pete Daniels Band.

Burgundy reg. at Windsor Hall and Wednesday Blue Bell, Saturdays and Sunday Club at the University.

November 17th.	The Burgundy at Clifton Ballroom, York.
November 24th,	Papa Bue and his Vikings at City Hall.
December 1st.	Burgundy at York again.

(On Wednesday Derek Lorrison sat in on tpt. He has an amazing knack of causing problems for the rhythm section. If he can't reach the note he wants in a solo he goes as high as he can and then changes into the key corresponding to the note he did manage to reach!)

December 9th.	Burgundy at City Hall opposite Ken Colyer.
December 11th.	Chris B. at City Hall.
December 13th.	'Going Down Ball' at Uni.
December 29th.	York again.

Two years of Jazz events 1961

New Blackshaw Band; Ted, Bill, Bob Penwarn, Ken, Brian Vincent, Joyce, Alan Blackshaw. Paragon Jazz Band; Colin (Spiv) Chapman, Bill, Trevor Hardy, Dave Tanton, Joyce.

January 11th.	Coming up Dance at University, 35/- Blue Bell every Wednesday.
	Regular sessions Windsor Hall / University.
January 27th.	Wally Fawkes at Windsor Hall.
	Bill in hospital for a while so played a couple of weeks with Ron Burnett on tbn.
February 16th.	Humph. at the City Hall, Burgundy played interval.
Feb/March.	Burgundy finished at Blue Bell. Dave Tanton (banjo) formed band with Spiv Chapman, Bill, Joyce, Alan Blackshaw, the Paragon Jazz Band.
March 3rd.	Sandy Brown/Al Fairweather at Windsor Hall.
March 17th.	Mick Mulligan.
April 18th.	Abercrombie still going, Tuesdays.
May 5th.	First gig at Windsor with new band.
May 16th.	I play gig at Abercrombie, tpt, from Merseysippi as guest.
May 26th.	Beverley Memorial Hall, interval to Bingo!

May 27th.	Astoria, midnight - 1.30am. opp. band from Sheffield.
June 6th.	Majestic Ballroom Tech. Coll.dance. (All this time the Blackshaw Band used to go horse riding on Sunday mornings!)
June 9th.	Bob Wallis, Windsor Hall - Blackshaw Band interval. (At this time band practices every week - often twice)
June 24th.	Scene we played 10-11.15pm.
September 5th.	Recording session (Philips?) Astoria until 3am. September 8th. Ted's last session as leaving to work in Plymouth.
September 9th.	Our wedding! Band played of course, Newland Park Hotel. Sessions at Blue Bell now Thursdays.
November 3rd.	Usual gig at Art College, Anlaby Road.
November 24th.	Band at Windsor Hall until 10pm., second gig at Ferens Hall 11-1am., another party at our flat until 3.30am. How did we stand the pace!
November 25th.	Another Uni. gig - all like zombies but crowd keeps us going, Mike Gordon played interval, very well, but fell off the end of the piano stool!
November 29th.	Rehearsal.
November 30th.	Blue Bell.
December 1st.	Windsor Hall.
December 2nd.	Band to Frank Bogdal's European Restaurant to keep us awake until jazz started at Kevin Ballroom, Market Place at midnight. We played opp. Paul Shep. Band. All to another party until 4.30am.
December 3rd.	University Sunday Club. Trevor Hardy now on clarinet, not Bob Penwarn. Think Paragon had folded.
December 5th. 6th.	Marist Rugby Club. (Reported to Jazz Jottings, Hull Times) December Rehearsal.
December 7th.	Blue Bell.
December 8th.	Opposite Clyde Valley Stompers art City Hall. Alan's car, from which we had unloaded gear, towed away by Police from the trolleybus stop. Cost us £2 to get it back!
December 9th.	Kevin Ballroom 12-1.30am.
December 10th.	University Sunday Club.

Note. Above run of gigs, one night off in twelve - and all of us with full time jobs as well.

December 15th.	Blue Bell.
December 16th.	Windsor Hall.
December 17th.	University.
December 18th.	Rehearsal.
December 19th.	Art College Ball, 8pm.-2am. Required to play the Valeta!
December 20th.	Rehearsal.
December 21st.	Blue Bell.
December 22nd.	Windsor Hall Fancy Dress Party, Bob Wallis Band, Ford's Hot Four (Bill, Spiv, Ken, Joyce) one hour interval to enthusiastic audience.

Bill. When Brian Vincent and I first played at Abercrombie it was as sit-ins for the odd number or two with the resident band, the 2.19. Sometimes we were able to make up an interval band of other musicians who had also come along to listen to the 2.19.

Joyce. I used to go to listen, but I didn't really know any of the musicians there, before I went away to College, They were in a different world to me.

Bill. Later on the 2.19 began to disintegrate as people like Chez moved out of the area - so did Glen Gibb, the trombone player. I didn't know these people all that well, in that we met them once a week. Eventually the band fell apart and Ken Ford and Tony Grunhill reformed as a band which they called the Burgundy. They asked me to play trombone and Joyce played piano. She spent the rest of her time with the Burgundy laughing at me, I used to take my shoes off when I played and she thought that was funny. It was a successful band in its own way and it lasted for a reasonable time. I took my shoes off because it made such a racket stamping my feet on the wooden floor. I'm a compulsive foot-tapper! We played a lot of gigs in various venues.

Joyce. One of the good ones was at the Art College which was on Anlaby Road, we used to play downstairs in the basement. These were equivalent to the present day pop concerts but performed in 1960 or thereabouts. The Burgundy Band had quite a lot of changes of personnel, I think one of the early trumpet players was a lad call Alan Sharp, who is still around, though I don't think he is playing any more. Eventually Ted Blackshaw joined the band he was with it right to the demise of the band.

The Burgundy Band played more and more gigs, we were regular at the Windsor Hall and Wednesdays at the Blue Bell, Sunday Club at the University and also Saturday nights at the Union. The band rehearsed every single week, Ken Ford had very definite ideas of how he wanted the band to progress.

Bill. Sometime about February/March 1961 the Burgundy Band broke up. When it finished Ted Tanton formed a band in which Joyce played. He was a fearsome person to watch, luckily he wasn't around for all that long. Then Ted Blackshaw took virtually all the Burgundy Band and formed the Blackshaw Band. We used to rehearse at a club down Cleveland Street, they've knocked it down now, unless it fell down after our practices! Bob Penwarn had come in on clarinet, band was in action about March 1961. There were all sorts of interesting bands at places like the Windsor Hall, the best one as far as we were concerned was the Sandy Brown/Al Fairweather outfit. There were other good ones, Mick Mulligan comes to mind. The Ted Blackshaw Band started playing on a regular basis, it was an excellent band and we spent a lot of time rehearsing unusual, at least for those days, unusual numbers.

Joyce. At this time there was so much jazz going on that some of the sessions didn't even start until midnight. There was the Kevin Ballroom in the centre of the Market Place for instance. These jobs were extremely difficult to do, the difficulty was staying awake! We used to go to the European Restaurant on Princes Dock side to keep ourselves awake. After the late Saturday nights the Blackshaw Band all used to go horse riding on Sunday morning, and if you can imagine seven musicians very hung-over at 9 o'clock on a Sunday morning sitting astride horses wending their way through Cottingham Village, it was a sight to behold!

Bill. It certainly was! We had changed from the Ted Blackshaw Band to the Blackshaw Band, the reason was that Ted had taken a job in Plymouth and left the band. The band was taken over by his brother, Alan Blackshaw who had started playing Bass with the band some considerable time before. The trumpet player who came in was Colin Chapman, commonly known as 'Spiv'. The change in personnel made a terrific change in the band, good as the Ted Blackshaw was there was now a different approach. Ted was slightly mainstream inclined whereas 'Spiv' was basically a New Orleans fan but going on with what was, then, the traddy scene.

Joyce. In the midst of these changes, in September 1961, Bill and I got married. The band played and everybody had a great time. As we couldn't afford a house at that time, we had a very large flat down Marlborough Avenue. This was the scene of many impromptu jazz sessions and band practices. Understandable enough we only lasted in the flat for six months before all the neighbours complained, sent a petition to the Landlord and had us evicted! During this time we would be playing as the main band at the Windsor Hall gigs at the University Halls of Residence, followed by a party which would usually finish in the early hours of the morning. Then we would all have a cup of tea and go off to the day job! It makes you wonder how we all stood the pace. I remember particularly at one University session an amusing incident which turned out not to be so amusing. The trumpet player always had his bottle of beer at the side of his chair. He would stand up, play his solo, sit down, pick the bottle up,

7

have a very nice swig and sit there beaming. It occurred to the members of the band that it would be quite amusing to fill this bottle of beer with liquid soap. Bob played his next solo sat down, took an almighty swig and was almost sick on the spot, he gave the most amazing yell, the audience didn't realise what was happening, the band fell about laughing. He wasn't amused one little bit!

Bill.   Not only that, he had dropped his trumpet on the floor and bent it and the idiot was threatening to kill us! Public confession, it was me.

Joyce. A regular interval solo at this time was Mick Gordon. I have never seen anyone consume so much drink and yet play so well. Finally, one session it really caught up with him. He finished his last number with one gross almighty flourish and fell off the chair. This tape is flowing a lot easier than it did at the beginning, maybe something to do with the bottle of whisky.... The Blackshaw Band was set to play at a Talent Contest, a very important gig for us, it was held at the City Hall. The car, from which we had unloaded all the gear was parked at the entrance to the City Hall. When we came out, after the gig, it had been towed away from the trolleybus stop to the Police compound. To get it back we had to fetch the Police who charged us three pounds to get it back again. At the end of 1961, during December, we had so many gigs that we only had one night off in twelve. This culminated in the final Xmas do at the Windsor Hall when so many of the band had fallen by the wayside that they had to put on a band called Hot Ford Four. The entire band consisted of Bill on trombone, Spiv on trumpet, Ken Ford on banjo and me on piano. The four of us were able to play a long interval, to an enthusiastic, probably drunk, audience.

Bill.   The Blackshaw Band at this time consisted of Alan on bass, Brian Vincent on drums, Ken Ford on banjo, Joyce on piano, Spiv playing trumpet, me on trombone and Trevor Hardy clarinet. I first met Trevor some years before this at the Red Cellar Club, which was in the basement of the Co-op building in Kingston Square. It was quite amusing because the band that used to play there were pretty awful really. I went to the loo one day and was standing there doing what people do and the feller standing next to me doing a similar sort of thing said 'Can anyone sit in in this place?' I said are you a musician and he said 'Yes, I play clarinet and saxophone, I've just moved here from Newcastle' Naturally I said that's O.K. just bring your instrument and play. It turned out to be Trevor who did bring his clarinet and played and he's been playing ever since. Eventually he joined the Blackshaw Band, and one way or another I've been involved with him for years. The rhythm section of that time was, I think, the best that I have ever played with, in that they seemed to have complete empathy with each other. They felt what the front line wanted and invariable it was the right thing to do. A superb rhythm section to play with, and I don't think I've played with a better one since.

Joyce. I think it was mainly because although the front line kept changing musicians, this rhythm section was together for about four years. Eventually we got to the stage where we didn't play as individuals and everybody instinctively knew what we were going to do next.

Bill.   All the bands at this time, for after all it was the trad boom, were playing lots and lots of sessions, though there were only two main bands in Hull, The Blackshaw Band and The Paul Shepherdson

Band. Between us we performed at all the major functions, including the Riverboat Shuffles which were very popular at first. Many out of town bands played on the Shuffles as well. One particular incident occurring at that time comes to mind, The Blackshaw Band used to wear black shirts and white straw boaters as band uniform, it seemed to be the thing to do in those days. We played a gig on Beverley Road, a 21st. birthday party and Ken Ford and Brian Vincent were staying at our house in Pickering Road, Joyce being away on a course, and about 2 o'clock in the morning, full of beer we all rode back, three up, on my motor bike! Ken was sitting on the pillion and Brian on the tank. We were wearing our black shirts and straw boaters and we were almost immediately pulled up by a policeman. He didn't think it was quite the normal thing to do and said Just be careful lads, we don't want any accidents, do we? A far cry from today's standards of crash helmets and all the rest of it. 1962 and The Blackshaw Band was still going strong, still rehearsing every Wednesday and playing at the Blue Bell every Thursday, still doing the University regularly and the Windsor Hall, with occasional sessions in York. In 1962 also, two of the band got married.

Joyce. At this time a pianist called Teddy Barker used to play in the Windsor Hall on a Sunday morning, he had his own trio at the New York Hotel. Martin Shaw used to arrive on his push-bike, pulling his double bass behind him on a trailer.

Bill. Talking about bass players, Glenn Shelwin who was playing on one of the many parades we used to have through the town fell off the back of the float - his bass was reduced to matchwood!

Joyce. One gig we played at Hessle Town Hall, we came out and Bill's motor bike had been stolen and we had no transport home. We did manage to get a lift and the bike was recovered at about three in the morning. In 1963 a lot of the jazz musicians began to drift into Clubland, because for one thing there was a lot more money in it.

Bill. There were plenty of big bands around, we went to see Duke Ellington play in Sheffield early on in 1963, one of the highlights of my life. The Blue Bell pub. had been been taken over by a massive red-bearded landlord called Clive something or other, he was a lovely bloke but nevertheless landlords need to make money and he wasn't too happy about jazz in pubs. During 1963 Alan re-formed the band I suppose, we both went to work with Teddy Barker, dance work, and eventually the band was without a bass player in fact we didn't have a trumpet player either. Ken Ford went on to guitar, Joyce carried on playing piano, Brian Thompson was on drums and Trevor Hardy on clarinet. We re-formed the band and called it the Midways Quintet. It was really a mainstream band. We played lots of Ellington music, which is what I would like to do all the time. At the same time I started playing bass and went into Clubland with the rest of them and for me the jazz scene virtually fizzled out for some years.

Joyce. In 1965 the Blue Bell packed up altogether. Round about this time the Embassy Club used to have jazz sessions, it wasn't trad stuff, people like Harry Chat and Frank Harrison played there. They were very good, more modern than the scene had been used to, the music was really completely different. Harry Chat formed a band at the West Park Club in 1967, a very similar outfit to the one that played at the Embassy. There had been a bit of a revival at the Bell, there were two bands playing there. One was the East Coast Jazzmen, which was

11

Blind Lemon's Band and the other one was the Bluesicians. The East Coast Jazzmen had got Colin Moore playing trumpet, he was a musician that I hadn't played with previously. Ken Ford played in both of these bands, he played banjo for the Bluesicians and bass with the East Coasters. There were bands playing at the Lady-le-Gros in Beverley. The Bluesicians were still together and now had Graham Galtrey on clarinet, Keith Stutt was on drums. In 1968 sessions started at the Haworth Arms on Beverley Road. These were very well attended with people sitting on the window ledges, sitting on the floor at the front. During last year we had moved the Hull Jazz Club from the Blue Bell to the Haworth Arms. The Blind Lemon Band was beginning to practice much more and was beginning to look like an extremely settled band.

Joyce. We tried to organise the Haworth with a proper committee and a set policy. We wanted more variety for the members,many jazz musicians who had gone to clubland were very glad to play at the Haworth where they could let themselves go with improvisation. There were occasional out of town bands and individual musicians at the Haworth, this was more or less the same policy adopted by the Windsor Hall.

Bill. During 1969, Alan Harmer started playing regularly at the Jazz Club. Alan, as you probably know is a piano player, a very fine piano player. At the same time Ted Tarling had got together a modern jazz quartet and was playing at The White Hart in George Street. This was really the time of the end of the jazz boom, people like Kenny Ball had gone into the clubs and were appearing on TV. In February we did hold a Jazz Club dance, at the Good Fellowship, but the snow was so thick right throughout the country that the Alex Welsh Band who were booked to play just could not get through. We had to manage with local bands but the evening was a great success. Financially we lost just £5 which we considered to be good. In April, the Alex Welsh outfit agreed to play at the Haworth to make up for not being able to get to the dance. This was a very memorable session, jam packed to the doors. We also decided if we can't beat 'em, join 'em, so Blind Lemon's East Coast Jazzmen went into Working Men's Clubs. We were amazed that at the end of some of these sessions members of the audience came up with autograph books! In September 1969, the band got to the final of the Hull City Council Talent competition. We were to play in the final for three minutes and Ken, who was camping in Scotland drove all the way back for these three minutes. We won the competition and the £25 First Prize each which we thought was an absolute fortune and then Ken drove all the way back to his little tent in the wilds!

Bill. I think it was £25 for the Band, not each! Every year the Hull Jazz Club used to run a River Boat Shuffle and in 1969 a band from the West Riding was booked to play. Unfortunately this band managed to get drunk and after the 'do' was over seemed reluctant to leave the ferryboat. This small problem was solved by the ferryman with a high pressure hose. It was a wet jazz band that went back to Bradford.

Joyce. In November the band was engaged to play at the Mayfair Indoor Casino. The reason that I remember this is that on this occasion I was wearing a wig, and as we tripped down this narrow staircase from the dressing room onto the vast stage the nails sticking out of the ceiling caught on one of my curls. My wig was whipped off and promptly picked up by the musicians walking behind me and plonked back on my head again and we went onto the stage in hysterics! One out-of-town session with the East Coast Band we managed to pile into our estate car six musicians, including all the gear. Coming down Bricknell Avenue, on the way out of town, a 14 bus came right broadside across the front of the car. Bill, who was driving, showed great presence of mind and drove on to the central reservation. Stopping so suddenly threw all the gear in the back forward and Blind Lemon got a knock on the head which caused him to say something unprintable! Bill drove along the grass, in and out of the trees and back on to the road again without turning a hair.

Bill. That was the end of the big jazz period in Hull, though jazz is still flourishing, the music went into a great decline. Influences. Who influences who? I think in trombone players there are not all that many for me, but Johnny Hodges was certainly one, he makes more of an impression on me than most of the very clever trombone players.

Joyce. I always wanted to play like Ronnie Parker in the Humphrey Littleton Band. Bill, It's 2 o'clock in the morning, we're going to bed.

Chesterman

O.K., well, how did I get interested? I joined the ATC at the age of 14 and to avoid square bashing took up the bugle in the band. This of course taught me the rudiments of playing trumpets without valves. At 15 I used to go to the NAAFI and listen to the Band Box programmes on the radio and some of the older Cadets, in particular John Lancaster, who was a drummer in the band, had an interest in jazz. The band that was attracting most attention at that time was Chris Barber and his band which included Lonnie Donegan and Ken Colyer, this must have been about 1955. In the band were one or two trumpets or cornets, most of them owned by the guys who played them. One day I found a battered old cornet that leaked like a sieve and it had obviously been discarded so I took it home and did a solder iron job on it, got the valves to work. Because I'd liberated it from the Cadets I didn't let it be known that I was learning to play it. So I taught myself, that's why I play left handed, I actually taught myself wrong, completely wrong, pressure playing, left handed and that's how I actually got started. When I'd mastered the rudiments of the instrument I owned up and got into the band. I could never read and in fact the original band couldn't read either but eventually, when I had managed to obtain a much better instrument, a trumpet from the band, I used to go to Cadets simply to have that trumpet. This was because I had started to play jazz. I actually got fired from the band when the Bandmaster who was a reader wanted to check the tuning one day and asked me to play a piece that he had given the band to learn previously.

I used to wait for them to play the tune and sort of busked, that's jazz for you!

Anyway, back to the influences. I saw the Barbers and the Ken Colyer Bands, Sid Phillips and a few other bands that were going around at that time, Clyde Valley Stompers, all these were at the City Hall, big dances because jazz was popular around that time. When I was about 15/16 I belonged to the Anlaby Youth Club and I started to try and form my own band. My first attempt was with a young guy called Harrison who was on guitar, a lad I went to school with. Malcolm Tiplady on clarinet, who I also went to school with, Stewart Tiplady on drums who was in the Cadets and Ron Burnett on trombone. This line up didn't really get anywhere so I started another which because it came out of the original mess up I called the Phoenix Jazz Band. The Phoenix had Ray Wilson on piano, he was the mainstay of the band. On trombone Ron Burnett, on drums young Mike Heep who, together with myself had been a choirboy at St. Mark's Church - he'd only just bought a drum kit and it was his first band as well.

In fact it was everybody's first band! On clarinet originally it was Malcolm Tiplady but ultimately he was replaced by a chap called Johnnie Scarborough. On banjo/ukelele Chris Morris. We didn't have a string bass player because these were very rare things in those days and originally (out of a skiffle type band which I belonged to at that time called the Skid Row Seven) my old chum from school called Ivor Bowen on a tea chest bass. Later, Ivor cleared off to London, so we didn't have a bass player at all. This band started to get work in the pubs and I remember playing the The Haworth Arms and Hessle Town Hall, but our main venue was Anlaby Youth Club, that was where we sprang from.

Let me go back a little bit now and tell you that the first live jazz I ever heard was the Crescent City Band which at that stage consisted of Al Jenner on the cornet, Billy Croft on clarinet - a very young Billy, just out of short trousers, Alan 'Drool' Walker trombone, Eric Dobson, bless his heart, on banjo, Eddie Anderson on drums and Brian 'Slow Drag' Kirby on bass. I'd heard this band during a Rag Day parade but I'd never heard anything like the way Al's cornet cut through the noisy centre of the city. He had a trumpet cornet as I recall, I was quite fascinated with it, it was neither a trumpet or a cornet, but his tone and the hotness of his playing was thrilling, as was Billy Croft's originality. That really got me interested in playing actually, that was the single thing and that was when I started to attend the concerts.

One of the bands that used to tour was headed by Cy Laurie and I started to get interested in classic jazz because that band offered me the best listening. The further development of my interest in classic jazz came as the result of a book by Max House called simply 'Jazz'. It was a very very biased book and made no apologies for it, but it did point in the right direction and hence I got into Oliver and Armstrong. It reflected in the records I could afford in those days, I was at school until I was 18. The Cy Laurie outfit consisted of Ken Simms trumpet Cy Laurie clarinet and Terry Pitt trombone. There was a succession of piano players, one that stands out was Ron Riverburn, before him there was a girl called Anne Varley. On bass was Stan Leader, Viv Carter was the original drummer and Tim Streeton played banjo. I'd been going to see Ken Simms play but the next time I saw the band they had a new man on trumpet and he was no older than me. He was called Bob Ray, that's not his real name but his stage name, and he was playing extremely hot. In my humble opinion he was the only person who equalled Al Jenner, who I thought was God - and still do incidentally!

I'm getting to a point now around 1956/7, The Phoenix Jazz had just started to get some work, we played at the Al Jenner venue when he was in Moscow, and we had a good following from the Youth Club, it was great for getting dates with pretty girls! Well, I worked with the band and suddenly found that they were getting gigs without me. I believe that Mike Heep, whose father drove the band around had taken over.

Anyway, there I was without a band so I started to try to put another one together, without much success. I found myself a steady girl friend and that was taking up much of my time. In the summer of '56 I went to work at Butlin's as a Chalet Patrol Man, in fact they got a few of us from Hull Grammar School and one or two other people I knew went up there. Graham Galtrey, Ron Burnett, Jim Swann, Dai Hughes (who is now known as Patrick Hughes, one of the foremost Avant Garde artists in the country) they all went up there and got themselves jobs as kitchen porters.

During the period of Limbo following the demise of my own band I used to go and listen to the 2.19, which in those days consisted of Ted Blackshaw, Keith 'Shunt' Smith, Glenn Gibb, Ken Ford on banjo and Guts Grunhill on drums. I think a guy called Al (Potton?) was on trumpet and Ted played the piano. I'd actually gone to audition for the 2.19, they'd lost a trumpet player at this stage. I was very kindly received and asked what I could play. This I was asked by Keith Smith who had been senior boy at Hull Grammar, he didn't recognise me even though I was in the same bloody patrol at Grammar School Scouts! Whatever, I didn't get the job and none of the band can remember my auditioning.

At Butlin's I developed a reputation for being extraordinarily lazy, unkempt and dirty. I grew my first straggly beard and refused to wear shoes, wandering about in rolled up uniform trousers and I was known as 'Jesus' or 'Lightning' as I had a habit of leaning on barrows talking to people. In my kitchen, working with me (I eventually became Head Spudman) was a guy called Ron Dunn who turned out to be 'Ron Dunn the Drum' He had a passion for the girl I was going out with and as a result, I believe, invited me and my girl to see the band he played with in Bridlington. The band Ron was with had two trumpet players, someone called Bud and Mick Pyne. Trombonist who led the band (or he kept it in line) was Chris Pyne, piano Gerry Rollinson and of course Ron on drums, clarinet Tony Dugdale. I sat in a couple of times with them but you can only do a limited amount with three trumpets. They did need a banjo player and they actually gave me a six-string to learn and then I started to play with them on banjo. We used to have regular gigs at the Hayburn Wyke Hotel, just north of Scarborough.

Quite a few well known musicians used to sit in with the band, I remember John Barry and Roy Castle amongst others. The summer came to an end and I had to go back to school. After I had returned to Hull it became more difficult for me to stay with the band even though I had the chance to play trumpet.

Eventually I was asked to join the 2.19 band, which I had always thought to be the No.2 band in Hull. Quite honestly, you couldn't have a nicer bunch of guys. When I joined the band they had 'Guts' Grunhill, Glenn Gibb, 'Shunter' (Keith) Smith, Ken Ford and a bass player called Johnnie Kerr. 'Shunter' Smith got his nickname when he went down to London on a trip and stayed at the same place as Bob Wallis. He got fairly drunk along with Guts and Bob was so concerned

19

about Keith's agitated reactions that he suggested that he might be a main liner - someone who injects drugs! Of course Keith was as clean as a whistle but Guts came back with the retort "No, he's not a main liner, only a shunter" and the name stuck.

The 2.19 held court originally at the Blue Bell but for some reason moved to the Abercrombie, the place has now been knocked down. I started to play with them and was really taught about the history of jazz. Guts was my mentor, he had a vast record collection and I learned by listening to all the names I'd previously only read about. For the first time I was able to make my mind up about jazz music, traditional jazz music. I enjoyed playing with the 2.19 but was still doing gigs with the Phoenix. Shortly after the Crescent City had gone on their famous trip to Moscow I was very surprised to see Eric Dobson walk into the Haworth Arms where we were playing one night. He asked me if I might be interested in joining what appeared to be the Crescent City. Naturally I said "What the hell's the matter with Al?" He said "We've had a disagreement, Al's starting his own band with Geoff Woodhouse and we're getting Crunch in on drums instead of Eddie Anderson". In fact, that was the start of the Unity Band. Drool Walker on trombone, Eric Dobson, Drag Kirby, Crunch on drums, Billy Croft and myself on trumpet. We used to rehearse and play for a limited audience at the Unity Hall on Anlaby Road, hence The Unity Jazz Band. Ultimately the band started to break up. Drool who had been deferred his National Service got called up; we got Ron Burnett as a replacement; Billy Croft went off to Newcastle Uni. and Brian Kirby went down to London to rejoin Bob Wallis. Before Brian went we had a recording session, somebody's got it somewhere on tape, Drag's last testament. Sadly he fell ill and died.

As far as I was concerned, that was the end of Unity and I concentrated on the 2.19 band with whom I had become very friendly, they were bringing me along very nicely. The Unity Band replaced me with Alan Peacock, Tony Dugdale came in on clarinet and they started in the old stomping ground of the 2.19, the Blue Bell. That must have been in 1958.

I left school in the summer of 1958 and got a menial job as a clerk with Sissons Brothers down Clough Road. Watching the Cy Laurie and other bands that had begun to tour at this time I got the feeling that I could probably hold my own with some of the musicians I'd heard, so I decided to wangle a transfer to the London office of Sissons. I told Sissons that my parents were moving to London and that I needed a transfer and I told my parents that Sissons were transferring me to London and in that way I went off. Somebody I knew as a good mate and friend, Jan Roustoby came with me and we eventually married. If it hadn't been for her I very much doubt I could have survived, it was tough but we managed to do it. I joined the first band in London, it was called Roger Spearings Jazz Band and it was pretty awful. Roger's dead now, his main place was playing in S. E. London and Kent. I was very lucky that almost every weekend I would get to sit in with one band or another. I particularly recall sitting in with people like Terry Lightfoot, Graham Stuart, Sid Morris, Acker Bilk, Sammy Willington and one or two other bands that are now just names in history. The band that I enjoyed sitting in with most was that of Cy Laurie, mainly because of its classical nature. The trumpet chair was then held by Colin Smith who had replaced Bob Ray. Then Ken Simms left the Acker Bilk Band and the job went to Colin Smith. That meant there had to be an audition for someone to take his place with Cy and at that audition I had never seen so many bloody trumpet players in all my existence! However, because I was known to him and one or two other people I got a private audition whilst all these other guys were sorted out. After this a few of us were offered a series of gigs with the band to see what was going to happen.

I decided that I was going to be a proper trumpet player after all, so I went to get my teeth seen to - I had a couple at the back that were pretty bad and another that needed to come out. Because I was a coward, when the Dentist asked me if I wanted to have an injection in the gum or gas I said I would have gas. I didn't want to know what was going on with my teeth, and teeth are a very sensitive thing to trumpet players. He explained that he could only do me on a Saturday if I wanted gas, he had to bring in an anaesthetist. So I rolled up on the appointed Saturday and remember slipping down the bottom of a well as the anaesthetic took effect and waking up again. The first feeling I had was "Christ, there's no pain at all! This guys the best dentist in the world." I went to turn round to shake his hand and I recall saying "Fantastic". Then I noticed I was a little bit dishevelled, the dentist was very dishevelled and the anaesthetist was climbing back out of the window. Apparently I had punched him through the window on the the balcony after going berserk! They hadn't done anything to my teeth at all. The dentist explained that I would have to come back the next weekend he'd give me a bigger dose of gas. I returned and when I woke up I found he had taken out nine teeth and that was his revenge! I went to do my audition with Cy and my three allotted gigs with him blowing air out of everywhere and, of course, I failed to get the job even though I'd been tipped by Colin Smith to get it.

Just before I auditioned for the Cy Laurie Band I had attempted to put together my own band. There's a history to this, and it goes back to about 1957 I was in the Spencers Arms, having a drink with Drag Kirby when Ronnie Burnett came in with a very tatty looking, bearded large sailor. This turned out to be Redd Sullivan who worked on the Union Castle Line and had docked in Hull. He'd spotted Ronnie walking through town with a trombone case, had asked him if he was a jazz trombonist so they had come along to the Spencers. That started a number of things, Redd was a folk singer and did a bit of singing with jazz bands whenever his ship was in port. He used to sing with the 2.19 and we did a memorable concert at the Y.P.I. Hall. On the same bill were Shirley Collins and Dominic Behan. I have cause to remember the Dominic Behan thing very well! I took my parents there, it was the first time they had been out to hear me play and it was a very very packed house at the Y.P.I. Anyway my mother (I'd warned my mother we were putting up some of the artists) watched all these strange folk singers and they got generous applause for what was a pretty awful Concert. The 2.19 was mind boggling bad but it was well received too. It turned out that the Chestermans had got landed with Dominic Behan, the brother of Brendan Behan, the radical playwright, as their house guest. I recall getting him home, opening the door and he just fell through it. I left him lying where he was, extraordinarily drunk. When my mother came down in the morning, there was Dominic and she confided in me afterwards that she wouldn't have minded anyone but him!

It was through Redd Sullivan that I made useful contacts when I was living in London and trying to form a band. That band was called Ches Chesterman's Scintilla Jazz Band. I was on trumpet, the trombonist was Trevor Adams, a clarinet player George Batty, a little fellow from Perth in Aussie, drummer Dave Edmunds and piano Alan Thomas. I had a banjo player called Jimmy James, who was unfortunately killed in an accident some years ago. We played all the usual London Clubs, Ken Colyer Club, Fifty-one, Cy Laurie Club, Humphrey Littleton Club (which later became Jazz Shows) and the Cellar, which used to be called the Skiffle Cellar. All the usual places in London in fact and all for little money.

Back in Hull one weekend I met Pete Deucher who had been running a band in Germany and was home to form a new one. He asked me if I would be interested and I said that I would. It was by far the worst band I ever played in before we went off to Germany we played in Hull and got the most awful revues. This was in 1960 we stayed out a couple of months and then it all fell apart. I subsequently joined Neil Millet's Band and stayed with them until February 1961. By this time, Jan and I had got engaged and we had actually set the date, March 18th. The snag was that Eggy Ley had offered me a job in his band which played regularly in Germany, he was very popular over there, and the tour was starting before our wedding day. However, there was a very funny incident which arose as a result of all this. I had decided not to say anything to Jan until as near as possible to the date that I had to leave for Germany. I actually broke the news to her early one Sunday morning, her reaction was "Well, I want to get married in Hull and that's what I'm going to do and that's what we ought to be doing." I had to agree, she was quite right and that's why I had been a bit reticent in telling her. So I rang Eggy to try to delay my departure until after the wedding and there was a whole lot of bartering, it started with Eggy saying "Well, I'll give you the day off". Jan pointed out that a day is not good enough to get married in Hull and he then said "Well, get married in Germany". Jan said "No" and then he offered two days off! When

I said that we couldn't afford the two fares back from Germany he offered to pay them. It became increasingly obvious that the forthcoming nuptials and the tour of Germany weren't compatible so I said "Look, Eggy, I'm not going to let you down on this one, but I'll find you a trumpet player to take my place in the band. A new trumpet player who is better than I am." With that, I immediately phoned Al Jenner who was living in a windmill in Skirlaugh, again that was that early Sunday morning and he'd just got out of bed. I said "Hello Al, do you want to go to Germany?" Without a second's hesitation he said "Yes". I said "Well, permanently!" He said "Yeh" So I explained that Eggy was doing a short tour of Scotland and that he could join them on the tour and then go off to Germany. As a result of that he played with Eggy in Germany and over here for two or three years and was very popular indeed. The funny thing is that when I rang he invited me round so I said "I'm in London". "Doesn't matter, come round"! Quite funny, but that was our Al.

The experience with the Pete Deucher Band had soured me for playing professionally again. I still hankered after playing with a really good band but I couldn't see it happening. Then a chance came when the Mike Daniels Band and The Steve Ryan Band both split up, out of that emerged the Alex Revel Band. This had Alex on clarinet, Alan Thomas, there he is again, on piano, Bob Sinclair on bass, Geoff Blackwell drums, Mick Clift trombone and me on cornet.

With reference to the wedding I was going to have, Jan and I finally got married. At that stage I was in rehearsal with the Alex Revel Band. We got the usual spate of telegrams including one from Colin Smith, Ernie Price and the Acker Bilk Band. We also got one from Alex Revel which we thought was very nice of him, but it turned out to be a

"Don't forget rehearsal next Monday" telegram! I stayed with Alex Revel for a couple of years, he was a strange sort of person and he tended to get up people's noses because management and band musicians alike got nowhere. In fact, we were the third band that the Harold Davidson Agency signed up, after Chris Barber and Terry Lightfoot. Eventually I handed in my notice but was persuaded, with a large dinner for Jan and myself, to stay on. Alex then waited a couple of months and fired me! That's jazz!

Around about that time the London Jazz scene was being worked on by the Press - they were looking for a sensational story about drugs. The bands had a very good idea of just what was going on in the various venues they played, as far as we were concerned there was little or no activity. Certainly no hard drugs, there may have been a little grass smoked. The only time we were offered drugs, which we refused, was by two guys who turned out to be reporters.

After this time I played with various outfits alongside such well known musicians as Wally Fawkes, Bruce Turner, Lenny Felix, Graham Bell and Sandy Brown. All this was very good experience and during this time I made the switch from cornet to trumpet.

During 1968 I formed my own band and we were fortunate enough to get work on the BBC. We tried to get a place on Jazz Club and to do this we had to play an audition. They asked us for nine minutes, three tunes of three minutes each and we did this, on one of them I did the vocal. Funnily enough, one of the tunes we did was 'Blues for Emmy Lopez' something I had written for the 2.19 Band. All the band were somewhat surprised when we got radio work after this because several well known bands had failed to please, amongst them Ken Colyer and Bruce Turner. We got work with Jimmy Young and on the Terry Rollins Show.

Then my job started to take me away from town, I had a house and a boat-house in Kent and it was getting increasingly difficult to play, and I actually stopped for several years. My job took me to Chesterfield, a brilliant jazz desert, there I actually got a band together which included Graham Galtrey. He was living in Bawtry and we played in Swinton near Rotherham.

The next few years were spent moving about the country. I had a couple of years back in Essex and then was moved to the West Midlands. I did some club work, in fact I went from playing very little to accompanying visiting American musicians such as Wild Bill Davidson, Benny Waters and Kenny De Verne. This got me listening to jazz again in the Birmingham area and I was asked by the Zenith Hot Stompers to replace their trumpet player. I joined them and we were together for two happy years, making records, doing broadcasts etc., playing overseas. Essentially, the same band with a different trumpet player and with the addition of a piano is still going now and it's well worth hearing if you get the chance. In fact that's why I left them, they are such good musicians and capable of so much originality that I felt that they were limiting themselves in the style of music that they played, following at that time anyway, some of the very well worn paths of British musicians. It just annoyed me that they were doing that and also that they weren't exploiting themselves quite as well as they might do commercially. I'm basically a salesman by nature and whereas it is impossible to argue that they have done badly because they were running the Midlands in terms of jazz, I felt they could do better and that being the case I decided to leave.

Once again my work took me away and in 1983 I moved south, to Hemel Hempstead where I now live. For the first four years my work was such that any regular playing was impossible, but I did play with one or two people, doing dep. work. In 1988 I joined the Pete Allan Trad Band. The Pete Allan Band has an ever changing line-up, for reasons which I won't go in to. His band was known as the Turnips because they come from Wiltshire and there are ex-Turnips to be found in every outfit in the jazz community.

To come right up to date, the day job collapsed and I am now a freelance musician and have applied for an Entertainment Agency Licence. I have every intention of continuing to play and am putting together a full time jazz band which will be a squad of musicians which I will need for corporate work throughout the country.

During the course of my playing I have come across several of the musicians I first knew in Hull. Cyril Stork, or 'Seth' as we knew him was living in Herefordshire with his brother Jim, neither of them was very well. Seth had given up playing many years ago but managed a couple of sits-in when I had a band down there. Avo Avison who played trombone became a Road Manager for one or two people then became a Publican. The last time I heard of him playing was when he was living at Randwick in the Cotswolds. I have played in his pub in Coventry, but haven't seen him for several years. John Collinson who was the banjo player turned into a pianist and went to live in Hastings. Bob Wallis ran a Jazz Club in Zurich for many years, sadly he died recently. Ron Burnett is doing very well in all his musical guises, living in York and presenting programmes on jazz. Eric Dobson has retired, though he attends the reunions and still can be seen around Cottingham. The last I heard, Tony Dugdale was running an architectural supplies shop in Islington, but not playing much in London. I think he has spent some time in the U.S. Alan Peacock went to South Africa, now returned and isn't playing.

Colin Lilley ran a hotel in the Channel Isles and is now back in Hull. I believe Geoff Woodhouse is in the States, doing rather well, he came back to the U.K. for Al Jenner's funeral. Chris Pyne is the avant-garde pianist par excellence. I was in touch with him recently, it is possible that we will be working together sometime in the future. I don't know what happened to Gerry Rollinson the piano player. Keith Smith's living in Cheshire, playing good. He does play good does Keith and Glen Gibb plays nothing at all, living in North Berwick.

A couple of disaster stories. I've already mentioned the first one, it was the gig I played with Pete Deucher, that awful band! Then when I was with Alex Revel we came up to Hull to do an all-nighter at the Astoria. The 'crowd' was either five or six strong. Talking of the Astoria and disaster gigs, starting out with the Phoenix Jazz Band, we played at the Astoria on Saturday mornings and to stand on that stage with all those fierce kids from East Hull, you got showered with Smarties and things, it was really embarrassing. Your shirt got covered with chocolate and sweets with things being thrown at you. They had a good eye, especially from the high seats.

Frank Courtney

Laurie, to think about writing a history of jazz in Hull, in my view is too pretentious. A history needs to examine origins and developments. To examine causes and effects, and I doubt if what you can put together will do that. The story of jazz in Hull or stories of jazz in Hull is probably more realistic. Anyway, with regard to my own interest in jazz land how that led to my involvement at one time for one period with jazz in Hull is as follows.

Possibly, like most people, my interest developed in my early teens, an interest in what I thought was jazz anyway, I don't even think it was jazz now. I suppose it developed from a liking of Glenn Miller records which led to a liking for and interest in other big bands. Certainly, by the time I was 18 the type of records I was enjoying and buying were Woody Herman, Count Basie, things of that nature, Bob Crosby and the Bobcats, a kind of orchestrated Dixieland. That's the nearest to jazz as we think of it now. Ted Heath was also another of my favourites at that time. At 18, like most young men I was called up into the Army to do my National Service; that was in August 1952 and by December 1952 I was stationed in Germany. It was whilst I was in the Army that my tastes in jazz broadened and moved away from the big bands to the smaller groups, these tended to be modern groups.

By the time I left the Army in 1954 my love of jazz was things like Charlie Parker, Dizzy Gillespie, the Gerry Mulligan Quartet. A few months after I got demobbed from the Army in 1954 an old school friend also finished his National Service, a chap called Alan Bateman so we got together again. Alan's interest in jazz had developed to an even greater extent than mine and it was certainly he that was the leading influence in our trying to find some jazz to listen to in the City of Hull. What we did find was the Crescent City Jazz Band which played in premises down Baker Street every Friday night. These premises were normally used as a school of dancing, it was a small hall, and every Friday night Lil Jenner was on the door taking the money, and inside, the band led by Al Jenner was providing the entertainment. In addition to Al on trumpet there was Alan 'Drool' Walker on trombone, Billy Croft clarinet, Eric Dobson banjo and Eddie Anderson on drums. I can't for the life of me remember who played bass and I don't think they had a pianist, though I may be mistaken there. Our Friday nights for the latter period of 1954 into 1955 were spent at the Crescent City Jazz Club listening to the traditional style jazz music played by this band.

Whilst enjoying the music, I never really had a yen to play. Alan however did, he bought himself a banjo and decided to teach himself how to play it. I know that at the Friday night sessions of the Crescent City Alan always used to try to get hold of Eric Dobson during the intervals to try and get tips and advice on banjo playing. Alan's banjo playing developed and eventually he started playing with a band on every Wednesday evening in a band at the Abercrombie Pub down Campbell Street. So I used to go along and listen to this, I can't remember what the band was called, I am pretty sure it was the East Coast Jazz Men. John Holborn was the leader, he played clarinet, a chap from Hull University called Al Potton played trumpet and they are the only names I remember.

There we were enjoying jazz, Friday nights with the Crescent City, Wednesday nights with the East Coast and then we heard of another band that was playing at the Blue Bell on a Friday night. So we went

31

along to listen to that and that band was called the 2.19 Jazz Band which had recently been formed, the nucleus of which came from students at the College of Art. Keith Smith on clarinet, Glen Gibb on trombone, a trumpeter who's name I can't recall, Ted Blackshaw on piano, I can't remember the name of the bass player - they called him Tulip, Crunch Thompson left and Tony Grunhill took over on drums. Ken Ford started to play with them about 1956 early 1957.

The 2.19 was extremely popular and in a lot of ways Friday night at the Blue Bell replaced Friday night at Baker Street. Although there was space for dancing at the Baker Street venue there was a unique atmosphere at the Blue Bell, this long narrow room, the band at one end and two rows of tables, everybody crammed in stomping away, enjoying the jazz. Of course, the 2.19 weren't the first band to play at the Blue Bell. What many people refer to as Hull's first jazz band played there in the very early fifties, that was the Bob Wallis Band. The person to talk to about this is Tony Grunhill, he was involved with that band. Bob Wallis came, like many musicians who have succeeded, from the town of Bridlington. I don't know why Bridlington has produced so many good musicians. Bob was on trumpet, another Bridlington lad was Avo Avison the trombonist, Guts Grunhill on drums, I think Cyril Stork played clarinet. Certainly by 1955 that band had folded up because Bob and Avo had gone down to London to make their fame and fortune.

There was jazz in Hull before that, I don't know about it from first hand experience, but I have heard tales of the Dixieland jazz that was played by a small group led by trombonist Harry Chatterton. During the war years, Harry led a band that played at the Fulford Ballroom on Beverley Road. (Officially the name was the Fulford Hall Dance Rooms, 72,

Beverley Road, F. Hakeney proprietor) In the middle forties there were large numbers of American Servicemen billeted in the area including a camp complex on the site of what is now the Lawns University Halls of Residence in Cottingham. I believe there were a number of musicians amongst the servicemen who used to sit in with the Chatterton Band down at the Fulford. A chap who used to live and work in Brough played bass for him in those days, he used to tell me stories of the wild jazz that was played by the Americans and how they all learnt so much from it. If anything, I suppose that was the start of post-war jazz in Hull.

By 1957 we had another group of Bridlington musicians who came through to Hull to play. They called themselves the Bay City Jazz Men. Mike Pyne was playing trumpet in that group, his brother Chris on trombone, Gerry Rollinson on piano, Alan Bateman who I mentioned earlier as playing banjo with the East Coast Jazz Men joined them, Ron Dunn was on drums. They were playing New Orleans jazz but eventually they dropped the banjo and began to play more Dixieland mainstream sort of jazz.

So we get to the beginning of 1958. I'd been enjoying myself, going round the pubs listening to jazz and it was at this time that I got more deeply involved with the jazz scene in Hull. It all started at 24, Hallgate, Cottingham. Now for many of us at that time 24 Hallgate was an open house, it was the home of the Nichols family, Kath Nichols, her two sons and two daughters. You'd think that with four kids, three of them certainly in their teens and twenties she would have had enough of a house full. But it was a big house and Kath, who was there alone because her husband worked abroad, encouraged the friends of her offspring to use the place as if it were their own. It wasn't unusual, even if you hadn't been out with any of her family to finish up there after the pubs had closed - 10pm. in those days. There was always a lively group there and of course, coffee.

It was on one of those evenings when the conversation got round to the fact that if you went to the Blue Bell during the week all you heard was the 2.19 Band, or if you went to the Abercrombie all you heard was the East Coast.

There was a need to develop a club in Hull that would cater for much wider tastes and not provide the music of just one band. Having had a few pints and feeling I could do anything I said Yeh, that's what's needed. I'll organise it and the place to have it is Cottingham. Cottingham should be the centre of jazz in Hull and East Riding. So, having said I would do it, I had to do something obout it. The obvious place of thinking of doing it was Cottingham, but bearing in mind the fact that none of the pubs had the facilities to present anything. What was needed was a room big enough to have space for dancing and room for tables and chairs. The main place in Cottingham at that time was the King Street Rooms, the Civic Hall wasn't built in those days. The King Street could hold about 300 but a regular booking was not possible. They had a duty to the community and a regular booking was out of the question. The alternative was behind St. Mary's Church, down the snicket. In those days it was called the Vestry Rooms, later it changed it's name to Arlington Hall and later still St. Mary's Hall, but then it was the Vestry Rooms. A church-like building with long narrow church-like windows and a very high roof.

The hire charges were moderate and the Haltemprice County Council, who owned it were prepared to hire it to us every Friday night, so that's where I decided it was going to be. You can't do these things by yourself, you have to collect around you a group of people to help you organise it. I suppose in this respect I was very lucky. The group consisted of Tony Gamble, Tony Grunhill the drummer Keith Smith of the 2.19, Mike Armitage - not a musician but just someone who enjoyed the jazz and Nicky Marlin, 'Nick the Fix'. When we wanted stuff we could rely on Nick to say he would fix it and fix it he usually did. Anyway, we got together and talked out the problems and decided that we wanted to form a club, but didn't want to call it a Jazz Club. We hit on the name of the Cottingham Rhythm Society and that original small group became the founder members. We held our sessions every Friday night in the Vestry Rooms. First thing we had to do was to provide a stage because then it was just a bare hall, well the main hall was bare, at one end there was a little kitchen and Ladies and Gents toilets. Nicky Marlin did his fixing, he fixed us a load of timber, Tony Grunhill took charge of design and craftsmanship and between us we constructed a stage, a portable stage, it very quickly became a permanent fixture in the hall as other people realised its uses. So by May 1958 we were ready to open, and open we did.

The 2.19 were our first presentation with the Hull University Jazz Band being the alternate group, playing in the half hour intermission. The following week we had the Geoff Woodhouse Band and the interval group was a group of way out modernists who called themselves the Freedom Rhythm Aces, trumpet, three sax and rhythm This band was made up from musicians from the military band based at Beverley Barracks, the band of the East Yorkshire Regiment. They were very good technically though modern jazz, the kind they played, did not go down all that well in Cottingham.

Anyway, the Club was a success, or the sessions of the Rhythm Society were a success. Two bands every week, we packed the Hall, we got on average 120 into the place, even though it was supposed to be 100 and everybody seemed to enjoy it. We had our first 'name' visiting band whilst we were there. The admission price for that was four shillings. This was the Bob Wallis Band. Bob had gone down to London but there had been a delay in setting up his band, due to his illness. Eventually he did get the band together and one of their first out-of-London gigs was at Cottingham. Of course, the local connections made sure that it would be a success. By this time, Al Jenner's Crescent City Band had moved from Baker Street to the Windsor Hall on Anlaby Road, this was a much larger hall than the one they had had in Baker Street. The Windsor would hold about 200 and I suppose we, at Cottingham, were in direct competition with them. What did happen is that it became apparent that the area wouldn't support two Jazz Clubs on a Friday night, the Crescent City weren't getting support and they folded up their Friday sessions at the Windsor. The Windsor Hall was then taken over by a modern group and became the 7-11 Jazz Club, run by Colin Lilley the bass player. He put a modern group together, some of the musicians from the military band at Beverley who had previously played as the Freedom Rhythm Aces, but that didn't take off and the club closed after a few months.

Cottingham was going from strength to strength and our main problem was that the capacity of the hall wasn't sufficient for the people who wanted to attend. We decided to branch out and open a club in Hull, but remember, Cottingham was the centre of the Jazz Universe so we opened a subsidiary club, Hull Jazz Club, at the Windsor Hall. This was in the Spring of 1959. What we did in effect was close

36

down the Friday sessions at Cottingham and move those sessions to Sunday night and run the larger capacity Windsor Hall on a Friday. We filled the Windsor on Fridays, using the local bands. The Sunday nights in the Vestry Rooms struggled on for about a year, I say struggled though they didn't make much money they didn't lose much and were a good training ground for up and coming musicians. But by the time we had paid the rent and the musicians there wasn't much left to go into the Club kitty and a hall half full or less than that doesn't generate a very good atmosphere. By the end of 1959 we had decided to close down operations in Cottingham.

Once we got to Windsor we were able to think big, we could bring name bands, visiting bands, out-of-town bands ,we weren't relying on the locals as we had done up until then. The first visiting band we brought in was the Alex Welsh Band and we quickly established a policy that every third week we would have a nationally known band. After the Alex Welsh we had the Fairweather/Brown band Dick Charlesworth and his City Gents and many others - I've forgotten more than I can remember. In 1961 I started going down to London two or three times a year perhaps for a long weekend, get around some jazz clubs, go and see the Agents. In 1960 when I was down there one of the Agents dragged me along to see a new band that had just been formed called the Kenny Ball Jazz Band. I quite enjoyed them and booked them for Hull. I looked at my diary as we had to book bands well ahead and it was going to be something like nine months later that we could fit them in, so we made a booking for them into 1961. By the time the band came to Hull, they had made a record of a song called 'Samantha' from the film 'High Society' and that record had got to No.1 in the Hit Parade. So, there we were, I had a contract for the Kenny Ball Jazzmen and was paying them £40 for appearing at the Hull Jazz Club at a time when they had a record at the top of the Hit Parade! They actually appeared three days after an article had been in the papers saying that they wouldn't play anywhere for less than £250. Many people who turned up on the night had read this and were amazed that we were only charging 10/- a ticket. We got more than 200 squeezed into the Windsor that night and probably turned away just as many. It was one of those nights when I wished we had the City Hall.

Another notable thing the club did in those days was to introduce the Riverboat Shuffle. The first one was in 1960, we hired one of the paddle steamers which at that time operated the ferry service between Hull and New Holland and sold about 650 tickets. The bands were The Alex Welsh, Geoff Woodhouse, 2.19 and at least two others and at 7.30pm. on a beautiful sunny June evening we set off from Hull Corporation Pier. We cruised down to Spurn, enjoyed the music, the company and the beer and got back around midnight. It was such a success that we did another one in 1961, this was included as part of the Hull Arts Festival. We had two main bands for that, Alex Welsh again plus The Bob Wallis Band. It was not such good weather this time, I seem to recall that it rained a lot, but we had a good time. The third and final one was in 1962, this one actually lost money because, unfortunately, everybody wanted to get in on the act and there were about ten jazz cruises in 8 weeks that Summer. As a result, none of them was successful. The Hull Jazz Club one which was in June got 350 on the boat to listen to Dougie Richfords London Jazz Men, supported by the Dave Mitchell Band. Something unusual, we also had Steve Benbow the folk singer.

The Hull Arts Festival of 1961 is worth mentioning, that was in June of the year, I think there were two weeks of artistic events in the city, heavily subsidised by the Council. Tony Gamble and I went along and appeared before the Arts Festival Sub-Committee and sold them the idea of having jazz type events during the Festival. As a result of this we organised the opening event, a concert at the City Hall of the Johnny Dankworth Orchestra. It didn't make money but we weren't bothered because it was guaranteed by the Corporation. For those who enjoy the Dankworth type of music it was a very good evening. A week later came the Riverboat Shuffle mentioned above and later there was a Jazz and Folk Song concert at the Bevin House near North Bridge, about 250 tickets were sold.

Another thing we did at Hull Jazz Club was to start bringing provincial bands to Hull and sending Hull bands to other towns. I well remember the start of this when we made contact with Grimsby Jazz Club. We met the organisers of that club in New Holland - I can recall shivering across the Humber one night and walking that one long street of New Holland in a blizzard of sleet and slush to meet these characters from Grimsby. The result of that meeting was that The Geoff Woodhouse Band went over to Grimsby and their resident band The Southbank Jazzmen came to play at the Windsor Hall.

There was a thriving club in Bradford called The Students Club, we had a couple of their bands over and sent them the Woodhouse in return. I think we also sent the Unity and the 2.19. We brought a good band from Doncaster to Hull, the Dave Taylor Jazzmen and a band from Leicester, The Trevor Jones Jazzmen, a really excellent band. So not only did we bring the well known 'name' bands to the city but also a good selection of provincial bands.

To my knowledge none of the local jazz bands made commercial recordings but certainly tapes were made of many of them. In the early days 1957-58 and later, Tony Grunhill would take his tape recorder to various gigs and hang a single microphone over the band. He has quite a collection of recordings by the 2.19. In 1959 I invested in a good tape recorder, I ended up forking out £120 for a professional Ferrograph and a couple of decent microphones. I used this equipment at Hull Jazz Club quite regularly recording visiting bands, The Fairweather Brown All Stars, The Alex Welsh Band, Bruce Turner and also some of the local outfits. Some records were made from these recordings, these were private recordings where the tapings were transferred to a disc. One of them was of the modern group from the Army Band at Beverley and we had some direct cuttings made on to disc for them. We made two recording sessions of The Teddy Barker Band, they played mainly for dancing on a Saturday night at the New York Hotel, but Teddy would draft in two or three jazz musicians, people like Ron Dunn on drums, Gerry Rollinson on vibes, Noel Flint on bass and play and record some modern jazz. One session was recorded at a Concert at Hull University and about 20 discs were made of that session, again these were direct cuttings, limited edition. A later session of a suite that Teddy had written 'The New York Suite' was recorded at the New York Hotel one Sunday afternoon and a limited edition of properly pressed discs was made from that. There were about 50 and they were sold locally. Another recording that was made about this time was of Kay Garner who sang with The Teddy Barker Band but I don't know if a disc was ever cut from the tape.

With regard to Jazz Clubs. I suppose atmosphere was all important, a room in a pub is a room in a pub, everything hinges on how good the music is or how much you are enjoying the music that is being played. If you are getting away from the pub room you need to have premises were you can create the right kind of atmosphere - in the normal state most premises, especially if you are hiring them once a week - are not ideal for a Jazz Club. When we started at Cottingham we were faced with this bare high room with church like windows down each side. So we bought a string of coloured bulbs, not Christmas tree lights but full size bulbs and our first job every week was to put these up. Wanting to get rid of the church like appearance of the windows we commissioned Glen Gibb to do huge drawings about five feet wide and fifteen feet long. These were mounted on canes so that they could be stored easily and when in position completely changed the look of the Hall.

The staple diet of Jazz at Cottingham was hot dogs and lemonade, we used to buy 20 crates of soft drinks every week. We had some girl volunteers in the kitchen frying sausages and making them up into hot dogs and we made as much money from them as we took at the door! What with the drawings covering the windows and the coloured lights hanging from the rafters it made for a good atmosphere.

It needed a different approach at the Windsor Hall, this was a much larger room, longer but not as high. Down one side it was all mirrors, I suppose to give the idea that it was much larger than it was. Again we used coloured lights instead of the bright main lighting of the hall and the mirrored side was covered up with strips of record sleeves. The sleeves were given away by the record companies for display purposes and we got them free. Another way in which we were, perhaps, unique in the country was in the use of a doorman. You don't see them these days but certainly in the fifties any function of class had a uniformed doorman. They were from the Corps of Commissionaires, I think they are all ex-Army men.

They wear a smart navy blue uniform with a Sam Browne belt and a white topped cap and are very efficient looking. Functions at The City Hall or Guildhall, any function that was anything had a doorman so we decided we were going to show them that we had a bit of class and hired a Commissionaire. We approached the Corps and they sent us Sgt. Johnson, he stayed with us through Cottingham and Windsor Hall.

When the Club closed at midnight it was very unusual to go straight home. Tony Grunhill had his flat in Pearson Park, the first floor of a large Victorian house, the important thing was that not only did he have this huge flat but he was also 'Mr. Ind. Coope' in the area, he worked for Ind. Coope and also ran their depot in Humber Street. So there was always a good supply of beer in the house, tins of Double Diamond and Long Life and we'd go back there, drink beer and play records. Tony had one of the largest jazz record collections in the area, maybe the largest. Most of the visiting bands went back to Tony's place at sometime or another. Another haunt for late night, early morning sessions was the Woodhouse pad at Ferriby. I can remember one occasion when The Wally Fawkes Band played at the Club and we finished up at Geoff's with Lenny Felix on piano and something like six or seven clarinettists playing. Tony Dugdale, Geoff Woodhouse, Keith Smith, Wally Fawkes himself and a couple of others who's names escape me at the moment, Graham Galtrey perhaps, but it was unusual to have quite a collection of clarinettists playing at the same time.

Clive Cross

It's Clive Cross, presently living at 27 Marshall Avenue, I used to live at 98 Hull Road Anlaby. My father was a fish merchant. Most of the friends I made in the early days were at Anlaby County Primary School, and names that come to mind and are mentioned later on are people like Michael Eastwood. Michael is still around, he lives in Cranswick. He played the trumpet and was a big influence on my early jazz career. I had to move schools later on, from Hessle High to Wheeler Street but I kept in touch with Mike. Although we had moved away from the area I used to go back to Anlaby Primary School, there was a good youth club there. Must have been about 1955. I'd studied the piano when I was younger but needed to get involved in some band or other if I was going to improve. What happened was that a band started rehearsing at the youth club. The trumpet player was Chesterman and I think that Tony Dugdale was with him. It was at about that time that The Crescent City Band had broken up, they had gone on some kind of a tour of Russia, I well remember the big send off they had had at Paragon Station. I wanted to get into the jazz scene and the Chesterman/Dugdale outfit needed a banjo player. I managed to get hold of an ancient type banjo and learnt it to G fingering but I never really got into the band until some time later - about 1956/7.

I'd met Paul Shepherdson at the College of Commerce and along with Mike Eastwood and Pete Sewell we used to go the rounds of the Jazz clubs in Hull. I kept practising the banjo. I had joined the Police Force as a Cadet in 1957 and met up with a man call Eric Pick, he was the banjo player in the Tivoli Orchestra at the old Tivoli Theatre. He had what I have now, a Paragon Tenor. He said Look Clive, you can use this instrument for as long as you ever want it He refused point blank to sell me it, has done over the years - and we're talking about a long time ago now - he's never been back to claim it. I've had that banjo since 1957, I am sure he still has the right to take it back, it was generous of him to let me have such a good instrument.

I didn't want to learn the fingering all over again so I tuned it to G and carried on playing, I didn't know any better at the time really! Eventually I went back to Tony and got into the Unity Jazz Band in 1957/58. The band played all over the place and we had a uniform of black waistcoats and trousers, white shirt and a red tie. If the Unity didn't have a gig we used to all go to the Cottingham Jazz Club especially if the Bob Wallis Band was playing there. I think Frank Courtney had something to do with the running of the Cottingham Club.

The Unity had a regular date at the University, we used to play there every Sunday night. We also used to play in the University Rag Parades. I remember one incident when I was a very young policeman, I was sort of buried amongst anybody I could hide behind on the back of a wagon. It wasn't appropriate for a young copper to be playing jazz in a Rag Parade, especially as there was the odd flour bomb being thrown. The local Sergeant, who was a bit of a tyrant, was riding one of those little motorbikes and got a direct hit of a bag of flour. He was covered all over with the stuff and rather unhappy about it, though he didn't know where it had come from. Then of course he saw me on the back of the wagon and said "It's you, you silly bugger". He took a very dim view of me being involved in the parade!

In addition to playing at the Uni. we also used to play at the College of Art on Anlaby Road whenever they had a do. The Unity had a large following who would turn up wherever we played. Saturday night was party night, the New York Hotel was a popular place to start the evening which might end up at the Green Door or on the beach at Aldbrough!

One night the Unity had to do a gig at a little village near York, it was probably Ron Burnett who got us the job. In those days, if we had to travel Alan Peacock would borrow his father's car, a big Humber Super Snipe. Somehow or other we would manage to get the band and the instruments into it, the double bass on the roof rack. When we got to the village hall there was hardly anyone in sight and we were advised to clear off to the pub for a drink.

When we returned there were still only a few people in but we went on stage and played a terrific session. We had brought a crate of beer back from the pub and really enjoyed ourselves. Then the guy who had organised the do came up and told us that he couldn't pay the band. We were a little unhappy about this and eventually he made a whip round and gathered up a hat full of change - better than nothing! One of the Band Managers - I use this term loosely, it was a way of getting in to places without paying - took the cash and disappeared into the toilet. When he came out he told us that the money had vanished from his jacket pocket. He must have had holes in his trouser pockets, when he took his hands out of them the whole lot of pennies and threepenny bits cascaded out on to the floor!

Driving back was quite fun. The car went straight on at a junction and I wound up with an arm through the bass drum skin, the radiator was

45

smashed to bits. Not many people had cars in those days, there wasn't the traffic on the road which we see today. Another of our friends and supporters had a beautiful Rover car which made him very popular. I think he would admit that he slightly mis-used this car, or at any rate was careless with it, leaving it out at night with no anti-freeze and doing the cylinder block in. Then he liked to drive it at Grand Prix speeds over North Bridge, nearly taking off in the process.

The Windsor Hall down Argyle Street used to be packed out on a Friday night. Apart from the local bands playing there I can remember Humph. Littleton, Tony Coe, Bruce Turner and Kenny Ball being booked. The Windsor didn't have a licence, soft drinks only, we used the Argyle Pub. across Anlaby Road. Our favourite tipple before we started to play was a Black Velvet, and cider. I don't know if it improved the sound, but everything seemed to flow a lot better. Then of course, when we had finished for the night there were parties here there and everywhere.

The Unity also played on the Riverboat Shuffles that were very popular at that time along with top 'name' bands. The shuffle nights were organised by Frank Courtney I believe.

In 1959 I became a policeman, naturally I was on shift work, this began to interfere, if that is the right word, with my social life I kept having to get a dep. in or dropping out altogether until eventually and understandably I lost my place in the band. I was only able to go and listen to them when somebody else was playing, which is upsetting to say the least. I was disappointed to lose contact there, if you like, in the progression that went on. I had to make a decision whether I was going to carry on as a musician or carry on in the Police. Hindsight would say that Yeh, the time has now come. 30 years in the job and I've got a pension and am financially quite sound. Where would I be if I had carried on in music   I remember Paul Shep. ringing me up from London, he'd got a place with Eggy Ley's Band and they were going to do a tour of Germany. They were short of a banjo player and I had to make up my mind about what I wanted to do, either resign from the force or stick in it. I must admit that I thought long and hard about this chance. I am a musician and I like to play and was always disappointed over the years when I couldn't. I've had to keep it as a hobby. Later on, from 1959-62 I only got the odd time to sit in when they were short and eventually my banjo went up into the loft. This was a shame really, I got interested again in piano but I had a job to do and sitting playing piano in a pub or wherever was not compatible with being a police-man.

In the mid-seventies I started to concentrate on the piano and became reasonably proficient at it again. My style changed a little. I learnt to play the electronic organ with the assistance of a fellow called Stan Brown. He worked for Gough and Davy's and I used to practice there. Many people think they would like a change from piano and that an organ is a similar instrument. It isn't really, there are two quite separate styles involved. When I became an Inspector I was lucky enough to win a place at the Police College. They had a big grand piano there and being miles from home I spent most of my off duty time practising.

My wife is a member of the Anlaby Park Methodist Church and the Minister asked me if I would like to play the pipe organ. I got in some practice and now enjoy playing the church organ.

But despite this concentration on keyboard work, I never forgot the banjo in the loft. Now and then I got the chance of a sit in with the band at Nellie's in Beverley. John, the guy who played regularly there wondered why I played tenor banjo tuned to G. I could hardly remember the G fingering after not playing for some time.

After an accident at work I was in hospital in Harrogate for months on end. When I came home I set to and re-learned the instrument with tenor fingering, in between times I got the odd offer to play. I was half remembering the G fingering, couldn't remember quite all the tenor. I was in the middle and that was quite hairy at times. I must thank Dave Peacock, he was very helpful to me during that phase I also got a lot of help from Trevor Hickson, the trumpet player. I sat in a few times at the Haworth when there was a Jazz Club there and slowly but surely the G fingering disappeared and I can't even remember that now!

The jazz days were absolutely tremendous. I learnt along with Mike Eastwood, I mentioned him earlier on. Mike was interested in jazz and we used to sit with an old wind-up type gramophone and play along with scratchy jazz 78's. Once you get the tunes drummed into your head you never forget them. I also learned a lot by playing with Paul Shep. He lived, at that time, in a small house off Newland Avenue. His father was a Humber pilot. He got his first drum kit and when it was set up in the front room you could hardly get anyone else in there! There was a piano though and we played a lot of music. Paul got himself a decent drum kit eventually and I'm not so sure that he hasn't got the same one still, he doesn't seem to have changed it over the years. I bet he wishes he had a pound for every time he's taken that kit up and down!

As with so many other players it was the Skiffle craze that started off many now jazz musicians. Our group got a week at the old Palace Theatre - long since demolished - along with other bands. Jim Dale was also on that week, I think he became involved in films later, and a group called the Vipers. Quite an experience being on the stage as a teenager.

One of the venues that I remember well is, now was, the Abercrombie. That was the name of the pub where the 2.19 Band played. I didn't have much chance to sit in there, Ken Ford was a regular attender and as you know Ken has been playing banjo very well over the years.

A character that I haven't mentioned before was Geoff Woodhouse. I played guitar for Geoff, this was before the time of the banjo in the bands. Geoff was a strange guy, he had a small Fiat 850 to drive around in. The difference between the backside of your seat and the roof on an 850 is hardly room enough for a guy 5'6" tall, but if you are 6' or in Geoff's case over 6', you tend to get a crooked neck or open the sun roof to get in! Geoff used to drive like some big buzzard sitting on a fence, head crooked down, when he drove that Fiat.

It was a fantastic time and I look at it now and see the youngsters of today and I wonder. I know we did our fair share of drinking but we were enjoying ourselves and giving enjoyment and entertainment to others. Do the young people of today get the same kicks out of listening (or being deafened by) the electronic music and the semi hysteria of the pop concerts? Maybe.

Eric Dobson, Banjo

My downfall began around the end of W.W.2 through listening to the American Forces Network programme (A.F.N.) on the wireless (as it was then known). Apart from the pop ballads and big band outfits they occasionally played the odd blues record which grabbed my attention. One that I remember was Basin Street Blues by the Charleston Chasers. About this time I became acquainted with two local characters also interested in jazz, Derek Woolley and Alan Broughton, who have become life long friends. Between us we collected the jazz records then available. Not many records had been issued in England and those that had were in short supply due to the war. However we did acquire a few covering a wide spectrum as the following list (from memory) shows:-

King Oliver - River Side Blues and Mabel's Dream
Jellyroll Morton - Winin Bay Blues and Oh, Didn't He Ramble
Bix - Royal Garden Blues and Jazz Me Blues
Muggsy Spanier - Dipper Mouth and Big Butter and Egg Man
Tommy Ladnier - Really the Blues and Ja-Do
Wingy Manone - Beale Street Blues - ?
Louis- Quite a few different titles.

Derek, who was a special apprentice at the Blackburn Aircraft Co. heard from someone at work that there was a jazz record club in existence. This would be around 1946. I know we both joined, but I cannot recollect much about it. (Compilers's note - This could be the record club started by Mr. Harris).

In 1945 I started work at Blackmore and Sykes, architects, of Scale Lane, Hull. Two of the assistants there were also jazz enthusiasts, Denis Crawford and Annie Cuthbertson. Denis had a large collection of records. Both left after a short time to go into the Forces. A few months after this Geoff Boanas joined the firm, followed by Eddy Anderson and Colin Lilley. Colin had a school pal called Al Jenner. It wasn't long before we had a jazz following which would eventually result in all five of us playing in local jazz bands.

Geoff was the first to become active by buying and learning to play trumpet. Colin, Eddy and Al Jenner followed and together with Geoff's cousin and a friend formed the Port of Hull Jazz Band. In retrospect the line up of this band makes strange reading- Geoff Boanas - trumpet; Don Fennington - clarinet: Colin Lilley - trombone: John Marshall - piano: Eddy Anderson - drums: and Al Jenner - banjo.

About 1952 the Hull Jazz Club was in existence, the leading light of which was Jim Stork. His record collection was out of this world. The members of the Club included most members of the Port of Hull Band and other personalities who would become musicians, i.e. Cyril Stork, Tony Grunhill, Alan Walker, John 'Bubs' Martin, Max Mallan, Brian Payne, Brian Kirby, John Collinson and Bob Wallis. The Club which would meet every Sunday in B.A.T.A. House at the corner of Beverley Road and De Grey Street to listen to records, also ran coach outings to Leeds to see the Bob Barclay Jazz Band with singer Deva Raphello. These were great nights out.

Bob Wallis who emanated from Bridlington and who had learned to play cornet in the Salvation Army was, with others from the Club, starting to form a band, the early line-up being Bob, cornet; Avo Avison, trombone; Cyril Stork, clarinet; Jim Stork, alto and washboard; Brian Payne, piano; 'Bubs' Martin sometimes played washboard and later Tony Grunhill played drums. Brian 'Drag' Kirby, bass and John Collinson, banjo.

The band developed and was soon playing regularly at the Blue Bell pub in the Market Place in Hull's Old Town. Eddy Anderson remembers sitting in with the band when on leave during 1953. The Bob Wallis Jazz Band as it was known was very popular at this period and played at other venues besides the Blue Bell. Cottingham Church Hall (Arlington Hall) and Wenlock Barracks come to mind. They also created some memorable nights when they joined forces with the Port of Hull Jazz Band for the Riverboat Shuffles which took place on the Tattershall Castle Ferry on trips down the Humber.

1954 saw a number of changes in the Band. Bob and Avo turned professional and went on to fame in London. Cyril had to leave as his job moved him to the South of England.

About this time Al Jenner, Colin Lilley and Eddy Anderson had left the Port of Hull Jazz Band and were forming their own band. The result was that over a few months the two bands amalgamated into one which became known as The Crescent City Jazz Band with the following line-up: Al Jenner, cornet; Alan 'Drool' Walker, trombone; Gerry Ross, clarinet; Eddy Anderson, drums; Brian Kirby, bass; John Collinson, banjo.

Early in 1954 John Collinson and Brian Kirby who I knew well from the Club turned up in my local, The Duke of York, Sutton. After several pints John managed to con me into buying an old banjo which was surplus to his requirements. The deal being that he would teach me the basics of banjo playing. I now became the proud owner of a banjo and a very slow learner. However, later that year John suggested I get my finger out as he had been accepted for a new post down South and the band would be looking for a new banjo player. So it was that I joined the Crescent City Jazz Band.

The band went from success to success. The trend at this time was for bands to play for dancing, not just passive listeners and to this end we left the Blue Bell and obtained gigs at the Baker Street School of Dancing and Vic Butler's School of Dancing in Anlaby. We did, however, miss playing in pubs so when the opportunity arrived we took to playing in the Abercrombie down Campbell Street. Now sadly no longer there.

In 1955 came a major problem when Gerry, the clarinettist who was in the R.A.F. at Patrington was de-mobbed and returned to his home in Rotherham. The removal of one out of three front line players is quite a trauma for a band which was just becoming comfortable with each other's playing. Our feelings were far from allayed when a youthful 14 year old turned up for an audition. So began the career of the fabulous Billy Croft. The band continued with hardly a hiccup.

In 1956 we opened the regular Friday dance session at the Windsor Hall, Argyle Street, a venue which was to run for some years after the Crescent City Band broke up.

As the following of the band increased so the venues became more impressive. To begin with we would do the interval spot at the City Hall when a visiting band, say Ken Colyer, came. Then we were asked to play at the East Park Ballroom and the Beverley Road Baths.

Eventually we were capable of filling the City Hall as the main band whilst Eddy would carry the interval by playing Skiffle. We were even asked by the Musicians Union to play at their Charity Dance. Later that year we got a gig playing at Art Saunders spot at Wood Green in London. We were driven in a Bedford van by Gordon Powell who had the unenviable job of trying to get sufficient petrol for the journey there and back, this was 1956 and the Suez crisis.

1957 saw the band's biggest success and its end. The band was asked to represent Britain in the World Festival of Youth in Moscow. We were a huge success and played to crowds of 100,000. The return was something different. Albert was becoming restless with the way he was playing and this alienated the rest of the band. Eddy had just married and was not as enthusiastic as before, but he did carry on playing for Al for a short period.

The rest of the band left to form the Unity Jazz Band. Eddy's spot was filled by Brian Thompson who had on occasion played for us in the past. What to do about a cornet player, that was the worry. Would history repeat itself? Yes, history did repeat itself - another schoolboy turned up for audition! So began the career of Ches Chesterman. All however was not plain sailing this time. Albert had no band but he did have all the bookings and was able to obtain personnel from elsewhere. The Unity Jazz Band was now complete but had nowhere to play - we even had to hire rooms for rehearsing. Worse was still to come, Alan Walker, who was playing at his best, was called up for his National Service - he never played again. Search on for a trombone - trombone found with Ron Burnett on the end of it!

Great news, a new venue - the band opened at the St. John's Church Hall, Clough Road. At last the band was collecting a following. The band was doing great things - PANIC - Drag Kirby has been offered a job in London with Bob Wallis. Can't think who replaced him. - DISASTER - Bill Croft off to University - no clarinet. Clarinet found, Tony Dugdale joins the band.

This must have been around 1958 and at this stage I decided to retire - for the first time. The Unity Jazz Band continued to flourish and I did come out of retirement to play with them again. However the talk was not about Jelly Roll Morton or George Lewis, it was let's play so-and-so by Acker Bilk. Well, somebody else can tell that story!

Albert Harrison

I've always been interested in music, from an early age in fact, but it was purely a twist of fate me or my brother Fred ever playing the bass. If you'd told me in the early sixties that I'd be getting on to a stage and playing any instrument at all I'd have laughed it off. That we ever started playing was only down to the fact that the well-known trombone player, Harry Chatterton, stopped playing regularly with big bands and took a job at Reckitts. That would be around the mid fifties. We got quite friendly with Harry, he came to a do at our house one night, and I was playing the piano. I'd taken lessons for a couple of years before I got married but after that I couldn't afford the lessons so I packed it in. I was a big fan of Harry's anyhow, so was my brother Fred, we used to go to all the dances where his band was playing and follow him very closely.

I could play one or two tunes on the piano, but only very slowly and after Harry had heard me he said "Why don't you and Fred get a bass". At that time, He said, they were crying out for bass players and he said that we'd both got a slight knowledge of both clefs - Fred could busk quite well on the piano. So that's where it all took off from, really. Harry said he'd get us introduced to a bass player, Noel Flint. He said "He's coming down to our house next week".

We went down to Harry's, he was then living down Chamberlain Road, Noel was there. Harry got this bass down which he'd got from somewhere down Holderness Road and put a record on and Noel started playing it. We've always liked music and my chin hit the floor when I heard Noel play, it was a knockout. We arranged to go down to Noel's once a week for lessons but first of all we had to get a bass. I had the good fortune to buy this one from Harry for £15 - that was with a cover - and going by today's prices he gave me it really, I don't think I would part with it now. We got two more basses, Fred went to Pat Cornell's and got two for £10, believe it or not, one of them needed stringing and was in a hell of a condition but Fred was a bit handy with woodwork at that time and he patched them up. So we got two reasonable sounding basses for £10.

We went to Noel's for lessons and as we had no car in those days we knocked a trailer together and used to bike down to his house with two basses on there, they'd never seen anything like it in their lives before I don't think! We went to Noel's for two years on and off, not regular every week but when we could and things started to take off from then. Fred got a job at the Transport Club with Trevor Bott long before I started playing. We used to go down to the MU clinics which were at the Windsor Hall and the West Park Ballroom. I can remember Eddie Grey going down there sometimes as well as Teddy Barker, the pianist. Eddie used to dash off arrangements for the front part like nobody's business and it was very interesting.

I eventually got my first job at the Trades and Labour Club with a chap called Charlie Smith - a lot of the older blokes will remember him - which lasted quite a while. The drummer was Jack Stubbs. I always remember The Trades and Labour because they had a big grand piano there with this lever lid open. When it rained the roof would leak into the piano, this ruined quite a good instrument eventually.

We got notice to finish and there was a few weeks during that time when I was away at camp with the T.A. Of course, when you lay off playing bass for a fortnight and come back to it you have to start all over again and I had huge blisters on my fingers. Round about this time Ivor Kirchin was on the go at the Locarno; I can't remember just what happened - Noel Flint was ill or something - and Tommy Vent stopped me at work through the week and asked "Are you doing anything Saturday night, Albert?" So I said "No, we've finished at Trades and Labour, I'm not doing anything". He said "Can you do Locarno this coming Saturday?" I said "You must be joking". "No, I'm serious. We can't get a bass player for love nor money. All you've got to do is go there and stand there with your bass and do your best". To cut a long story short, I went along and in those days had no amplification at all and I was absolutely petrified. Eddie Grey was on piano and he sorted the music out. They played too fast for me to follow it in any case and I was just delving into the unknown really. I don't know if a lot of people remember the revolving stage there, we were all set to go on after the trio that played there first. The stage started to revolve and I heard the music start. I was standing too near the edge with the bass and as we started to come round it caught the wall and all the music tippled off the stand. I'll always remember Eddie, he shot up and gathered all the music back in one hand and got it all reasonably sorted and was back in position by the time we got to the front!

We started playing, I'd never experienced anything like that before, I just felt like a non-league player getting thrown into an International. I was absolutely petrified, I played the best I could and this blister I had burst within about half an hour, my finger was just numb. We enjoyed it, but they were playing big band numbers, I had no amplification and was playing as hard as I could and somehow got through the night. When I got home, I don't think I slept a wink all night, the tunes were flashing through my head and I was soaked in sweat.

I'll certainly remember that job until my dying day! After that job, there was another one cropped up at the Skyline with Bob Grant and I had the good fortune to get work there. I stayed at the Skyline for 2 - 3 years and had some marvellous times. One particular trumpet player a lot of musicians will remember, Jack Barker, he was a right character. We had some great nights at the Skyline.

After the Skyline, I moved to the Docker's Club down Posterngate. Bernard Downs was on piano and Pete Robbie on drums. Bert Hudson was there originally, I remember Alf Rivetts playing there on a Sunday dinner sometimes. I was there for two or three years and then I went to the Old Brunswick Club off Waterloo Street where brother Fred had been playing. He had moved to the Wellington Club and I took over his job. One particular strange incident happened whilst I was playing at the Brunswick, during the New Year's Eve do my E string went on me as I was playing - frightened me to death! By an amazing coincidence brother Fred had also had an E string go on the same night. The chances of this happening are millions to one.

While we were playing with Bob Grant at the Skyline we used to get a few gigs at the Station Hotel. One night, I won't say whose dance it was because I don't want to embarrass the bloke, there was a large florid gent who had been busy organising all afternoon. By the look on his face he'd been sampling a few stirrup cups and had a huge bloom on. In those days they had a prefabricated stage at the Station Hotel, a little wooden thing with a carpet flung over it. We hadn't been playing long when the florid gent. came on to the stage to make an announcement. Whoever had put the stage together had left the carpet overlapping the supports by six inches, this huge bloke stood on the carpet and there was nothing under it. He stumbled on to the stage, piled into the drums, turned round, scowled at the carpet and if looks could kill that carpet would have gone up in smoke! During the night a girl soprano got up to sing, she was a very good singer too, there was a deathly hush. Then a waiter came down to serve at a table, fell over something sticking out of the stage and the tray full went all over her! Absolutely ruined the song! A night of disasters. To cap it all, the young lady got up to sing 'God save the Queen' and the large florid man would insist on accompanying her in a deep loud voice that was as flat as last nights flagon of cider. When we were packing the gear up another bloke came up to the stage and gave out the most vicious dressing down I have ever heard. He was obviously one of the Directors and he tore the poor drunk to shreds.

During the time I was playing at Docker's there was a stripper on, it was Sunday dinner. All of a sudden police came on from both sides of the stage, stopped the show and cleared the place. It never did any good after that, it seemed to go downhill rapidly. I remember a bloke outside, they were putting him in the Police van, his mate was saying they shouldn't have carted him away so they chucked him into the van as well! Bit of rough justice but I suppose he asked for it.

Trombonists seem to have figured largely in my career as a bass player, it was through the trombonist Harry Chatterton that me and brother Fred got started. When I was playing with the Society Jazz Band at the Crest, Bob Penwarn got Roy Williams down and we played a concert there, Roy came down a couple of other times, to the Station Hotel and the Shoulder of Mutton, he was a very nice bloke. Trevor Hickson booked the one and only George Chisholm for a gig at the Maybury (now pulled down) and also Len Hanson and Maurice Sulworthy. Great nights of music. But that's all water under the bridge now.

John 'Blind Lemon' Holborn

I left school in 1946 and commenced work as a Telegraph Boy at the princely wage of £1.2s.3d. a week. I was interested in all kinds of music, I played the banjo and the mouth organ, known as a harp to us afficianados. I believe that it was the hearing of Twelfth Street Rag that was the catalyst for my love affair with jazz. I bought an old metal clarinet, thought I was the only clarinet player in the world, then I came to my senses and set out to learn to play! I was lucky enough to go to Derek Glover, an Inspector in Hull City Police and a member of the Police Band. He was not only a fine clarinet player but was also a viola player in the Hull Philharmonic. I couldn't have found a better teacher. Inspector Glover left the area, and I was referred to Bert Brooks on Spring Bank. He was a great teacher for me, he was also one of the Police Band musicians. I played with Band for some time, there were five clarinettists in the Band and I was the fifth! This gave me a good grounding in the theory of music and I set about getting some experience in playing jazz. At first I had a difficult time in trying to form a band from any musicians who were around. I must admit to vague memories of 'crossover' music. I played guitar, I remember fondly, with one of the first rock, or rock and roll bands in the area. This was at the newly-built Ganstead public house on Holderness High Road. I had heard that there was a band playing at the Blue Bell. One evening I took my metal clarinet and went looking for jazz! Bob Wallis was the leader of the embryonic New Orleans Band and the Landlord of the Blue Bell had loaned him the money to buy a trumpet. He had a cornet, for at that time he played cornet in Bridlington. That was one of the best times of my life. I was surrounded by like-minded musicians and lived for just one thing only, jazz. It was a great time. Bob Wallis was in all senses the leader. He had infectious humour, a gravelly voice. He was held in great affection by all those around him. He it was that gave everybody a nickname, I got Blind Lemon; after the great partially-sighted Blind Lemon Jefferson. Alan Walker on trombone got Drool, I could never work out why, Brian Kirby on bass got Drag. Bob decided that he would go to London to seek his fortune and took with him any member of the band who wished to go. I was faint hearted, I'm afraid. He went to the Smoke and the rest is history. I remember about this time a young ex-Army clarinettist called Bernard Brook. I stayed in Hull and formed a band called the Riverside Jazzmen and played round the Clubs a while, in fact from about 1958 to 1962, and then the old bug hit me again. I continued playing with other bands until I formed the East Coast Jazzmen in September 1967. To get the record right, the original members were Colin Moore on trumpet, Bill Cater on trombone, Joyce Cater on piano, Martin Wynn on banjo, Brian Hairsine on bass and Michael Wright on drums. I took the clarinet seat.

The band was resident at the Hull Jazz Club every Tuesday, the Club was the centre of most jazz in the area. The other resident band were the Bluesicians, that was Trevor Hickson's Band. They formed a very good contrast. The Hull Jazz Club did some good work for jazz in the area, it eventually began to stage national and international jazz at the Haworth Arms. It also encouraged local budding and established bands. The Hull Arts Centre of course, as it was then, it later became the Humberside Theatre and later still the Spring Street Theatre, also presented local and national bands.

City Hall, Hull 1956, Al and Lil Jenner Backstage

The Jenner Band, City Hall, Hull 1956

Brian 'Slow Drag' Kirby,
Al Jenner's Band Concert,
City Hall, Hull

Eddie Anderson at Al Jenner's Band Concert, City Hall, Hull

Eric Dobson, Al Jenner's Band Concert, City Hall, Hull

May 1956 *Drums* Eric Wright, *Bass* John Carnazza, *Trumpet* Trevor Hickson,
Piano Gordon Finlay, *Altos* Bernard Collinson, Lenny Rangely,
Baritone Gordon Roberts, *Alto* Ev Snowden

Tommy Fisher Band 1956-57

Majestic Ballroom, Witham, 1961, Leon Riley *Vocals*, Gordon Finlay *Piano*, Harry Chatterton, *trombone*, John Carnazza *Bass*, Gordon Roberts, *alto*, Don Murray *Drums*

Adelaide Club 1957 *Trumpets* Trevor Hickson, Billy Clutterbrook, *Piano* Eric Smith, Bass John Carnazza, *Drums* Sammy Walsham, *Vocals* Jimmy Flint

Bluebell Inn, Market Place 1967-1968 Harry Chatterton, *trombone*, Sandy Brown *clarinet*, Ken Ford, *bass*, Billy Clutterbrook, *trumpet*

"Blind Lemon's" East Coast Jazzmen 1965

Geof Woodhouse

David "Sam" Langford, Secretary of the Training College
Jazz and Blues Society 1966-69

J. J. 1988

Alan Hunter 1988

Jazz at the Billy

Dave Mitchell 1988 Jazz at the Billy

Jazz at the Marina 1990 L. Dex *(Left)* Roger Cameron
(Centre) and John "Blind Lemon" Holborn *(Right)*

The Hull Jazz Club at the Haworth Arms had some organisation, it was run by a committee and dedicated to promoting jazz in the Hull area and in this it was very effective. We certainly had a ball. It is hard to tell what the future holds for jazz, it is being played more in other countries than in its birthplace, New Orleans. I am currently playing clarinet with a very earthy sevenpiece called the 19-19 Jazz Band at Nellie's in Beverley. So difficult to find musicians that are compatible, maybe that sounds unctuous, but it's true.

If I had to lay it on the line, I would have to give my own personal definition of New Orleans style as follows. Jazz has conflicting functions, it must entertain, it must be audibly and visually agreeable but it must also be aesthetic. All that a musician with integrity can do is to weave the tortuous path between the two. The same dilemma faces all musicians of course, from the Classics to the current popular music. I confidently believe that there are musicians involved in all music who are managing to tread the path though commercialism is the biggest obstacle, no doubt about it. Remember the old song title 'Money is the Root of All Evil' There is a little game that can be played by changing the accents on the words of song titles. I've always wondered what part of her anatomy is a lady's Now - you know the old melody 'I wonder who's Kissing her Now' That's all folks, see you around.

Alan Hunter

I first got interested in jazz in the mid 1950's with half a dozen school pals over in York. We listened to a lot of people on record like Bunk Johnson, George Lewis, Benny Goodman, Jack Teagarden, Muggsy Spanier and of course the incomparable Louis Armstrong.

Closer to home, we went to see Chris Barber and Humph as often as possible. Eventually we put together a band with a trad line up, including a tea chest bass (we were perpetually skint in those days except for the trumpet player, whose parents must have been great jazz enthusiasts. As well as a trumpet, he also had a flugelhorn, soprano sax and valve trombone).

We performed here and there in and around York for a couple of years before we all went our separate ways. I played the banjo and guitar at that time. Our only claim to fame was that we actually shared the stage at the Old Rialto in York with no less a celebrity than the great John Barry, whose father owned the place, and who played the trumpet with a group known as the John Barry Seven before his meteoric rise to fame and fortune as a James Bond accomplice.

I had a spell as a student in Manchester after that, and didn't play much except once at the Ardwick Hippodrome during a fund raising event. Several of us played in the wrong key, but nobody seemed to mind, and anyway the Tiller Girls were nice to look at close up.

In 1964, my job took me to Hull to work for the City Council, where I ran into a fanatical chap in the Planning Department called Geoff Boanas, who played the cornet with tremendous power and not a lot of finesse. He'd played some years earlier with an outfit called the Port of Hull Jazz Band, but that was before my time. Quite soon, I found I had bought another banjo, and was down to play at the Club Penguin in Anlaby Road. It struck me as odd firstly that the musicians had to pay to get in, which Bill Cater grumbled about, and secondly that Geoff didn't bother to tune up - he just blew. Bill wasn't overjoyed about that, either. John Holborn was the clarinettist but I can't remember much else about it. Amnesia has its advantages.

About that time John seemed to be out of sorts with some of the other East Coast Jazzmen, the only regular band in the area. People told me this was a seasonal occurrence, and so Geoff and me ended up playing for a while at the Haworth in John's band. The Haworth then had a magnificent barrel vaulted ceiling, which was good acoustically, until some philistine replaced it with a more modern suspended thing which completely ruined the place. Soon after, John got his own band back together. Geoff and me were allowed to find our own level, as it were, and sank from view, but not before we'd spotted a really amazing bloke in the audience called John Whitehead, who knew all about Bunk, George Lewis and especially Ken Colyer, and who sported a very impressive set of whiskers which we thought would look good as a backdrop to a banjo. I'd, by then, become interested in the trombone. Life wasn't long enough to try for the Teagarden style, but then the much less demanding tailgate approach seemed a more appropriate one to go for anyway.

Without too much persuading, our new recruit took up the banjo, and in quite a short time became an authority with a notable collection of very high quality instruments. Geoff talked an old acquaintance called John Bottery into turning up to play the clarinet at John- the-banjo's house, where the four of us used to meet once a week to build up some sort of repertoire. I remember John-the-clarinet had a terrific command of the instrument even then, although he played from the dots and was pretty unfamiliar with any sort of improvisation. (Now listen to him!)

After a few months, Geoff had found a drummer and a bass player, but even better, a fantastic venue - Nellie's in Beverley, where we began to play in 1977. This ancient and grotty pub was absolutely perfect for jazz. The old sisters who ran the place opened up a room which had been locked up for the previous fifty years: gas lighting, wooden floorboards and the most terrific acoustics. Real Ale too.

True to form, Geoff regularly drew on the power of his personality to recruit other members of the audience to join him as the need arose. His victims included Brian Stowe (drums), a former racing cyclist with the requisite leg power and devotion to the New Orleans style. Ron Burn (piano), a quiet and efficient Geordie, and Terry Swanborough who came in on bass after we had lost Frank Williams so tragically. By an ironic twist of fate, John Bottery moved on to greater things, and was replaced by none other than John Holborn, who by then had fully recovered from his encounter with Ken Colyer.

Not many people know about this, but as I was there at the time, perhaps the truth should be told. Years earlier, we had all gone to hear Colyer in a nice pub in Bridlington called the Londesborough. At the end of the evening, we went to have a natter with the musicians as they packed up. Ken had left his cornet on a chair and Blind Lemon lived up to his name by knocking it noisily and rather publicly to the floor...Ken Colyer sticks in my mind as a man of few words, most of them expletives. It's the only time I remember John being rendered speechless.

The Londesborough by the way was another venue rich in character. A man used to bring round a dustbin at the interval, full of hot jacket potatoes and - wait for it - black pudding. Aarrgghh!! Once, I saw Monty Sunshine play there. A drunk at the back asked him to play "Stranger on the shore". He didn't seem too keen. I don't suppose it's the first time it's happened. The moral of all this is that musicians are long suffering people. But so are audiences, especially at Nellie's. We tell them to bring their friends. Quite a lot bring their enemies...

Dave Mitch

How did I first become interested in jazz? Well, I suppose it all started for me when I was called up for National Service in 1949. I went in to the R.A.F. and at that time I knew nothing about music or jazz and had no interest in it either. I had played a cavalry trumpet in the ATC band but I really wanted to be a drummer like everybody else. I used to practice with batons of wood on the bench at Reckitt's saw mill where I worked. After spending a couple of weeks at RAF Padgate I was posted to West Kirby to do my basic training and I clearly remember marching with a lot of other recruits from the Railway Station to the strains of Colonel Bogey played by the voluntary band of West Kirby. Afterwards I was told that playing trombone in that band was Keith Christy, later to be in Humphrey Littleton's outfit.

Following West Kirby I was posted to RAF Wellsbourne to do trade training in photography. They had a voluntary band there and I became a member of the band playing side-drum. After trade training I was posted to RAF Mildenhall, and this is where I became really interested in music. The reason for this was because the Number Three Regional Band of the RAF was stationed there, as well as the voluntary band which I joined, again playing drum. We used to rehearse in the Number Three Band's bandroom. One evening when we were there for rehearsals, the solo cornet player of that band was playing a trumpet, practising, it really impressed me. I'd never heard anyone play the trumpet like that and from then onwards I thought I must play the trumpet. At that time all juke boxes were playing tunes like 'My very good friend the milkman' by Fats Waller, 'Fine brown frame' by Nellie Lutcher and the Nickelodian song. Harry James was very big at that time, he had a hit with 'Carnival of Venice' and it impressed me very much. I enjoyed listening to that kind of music. I had a word with the bod that ran the band, he was a full-time bandsman and told him I wanted to start playing trumpet. Of course he said 'Can you blow one'? and I told him I had played one in the ATC Then I decided I must get myself a trumpet with three valves. The next time I went home on leave I had a word with the lady next door, her brother George Cox was a well known sax player in the Hull dance band circles. He also happened to be a Club Check Agent and he got me a trumpet for ten pounds, second hand from Paragon Music Stores. He said to me It's a good trumpet, Dave, I've tried it myself, it works perfectly . Well, I struggled with this trumpet for two or three weeks and got nothing out of it but strangled sounds so I decided to take it to bits and see if there was anything wrong inside it. Well, of course, you know that with a trumpet the three valves are numbered, these were all in the wrong places. As soon as that got sorted out I started to improve.

Eventually I was posted to RAF Marham in Norfolk and there I met a chap who played the cornet, he was interested in jazz. He had a good collection of records so I was able to hear quite a lot of jazz. Also in those days there was a Jazz Club programme on the radio, it was often recorded from the Cook's Ferry Inn and featured Freddie Randall. During all this time I was trying to learn how to play the trumpet and read music, but without much success.

I was demobbed in 1951 and about that time a lot of old jazz was being released on Parlophone 78's. I bought some of these records such as

Louis Armstrong's Hot Five, Bunk Johnson, Sydney Bechet and The New Orleans Wanderers. My father used to have one of the old type wind-up gramophones and I used to adjust the speed of the record and attempt to play along with it. For a while during this period of time I took a job as sea-side photographer at the great metropolis of Withernsea and it was while working there that I met Alan Harmer who was working on the roundabouts during the day and playing piano in Billy Barber's pub in the evening. I made friends with Alan and we have been great pals ever since.

After I had been out of the RAF for a year, I found myself out of work and decided to try to rejoin as a bandsman. I finished up in the 2nd. Parachute Regiment Band. Of course, having been in the forces before I was used to marching and drilling so the Bandmaster put me in the Marching Band. The very first job I went on was at the Tower of London and I hadn't got a clue on how to march and play the cornet as well! I was in just to make the numbers up really.

I soon found out that there was a Jazz Club just a bus ride down the road at a pub called the White Hart in Blackwater. We used to go and listen to the jazz on a Saturday night. Aldershot only being a short train ride from London I could often travel down to town. One of the places I went to was called Studio Fifty-One down Gt. Newport Street off the Charing Cross Road. Ronnie Scott played there a lot before he had his own club and I must be one of the very few people to remember seeing Benny Green playing sax. In those days it was quite OK to walk round Soho, I don't think there were so many evil people around as there are now. We also went to the Cy Laurie Club at the back of the Windmill Theatre and I remember the first time we went in there, down the steps to the cellar. The people were very sociable and greeted us like long lost friends. I can't really remember much about the music but there was a big fat bloke with a ginger beard playing trumpet, I still don't know who he was, perhaps somebody else will be able to enlighten me on that. Another place we went to during those days was the Flamingo Club, I don't think it reigned very long because shortly after that Ronnie Scott's Club opened.

I had a good friend at Aldershot, Jimmy Wallace, who came from Dundee. He was a very versatile musician, playing clarinet, sax and piano. We used to do a little busking in the pubs and apart from the beer that used to get sent up we got paid 25 shillings. Being in the Army we were usually broke and the twenty five bob would provide us with a couple of mixed grills at four shillings a head, not to mention a pint or two.

The melody Maker newspaper was always interesting, one week I saw an item about an "Eight Pound a Week Salesman Gets New Job" This was the start of the career of Kenny Ball. Sid Phillip's band had needed a replacement for Cyril Ellis and Freddy Randall had recommended Kenny. I saw the Phillips Band at the Aldershot Hippodrome, that was the first time I saw Kenny play, I was also very impressed by trombonist Norman Cave, a really magnificent player.

Being in the Army, when I came home on leave I had no real friends. Naturally I looked for jazz in Hull and found it at the famous Abercrombie in Campbell Street. Al Jenner with his Crescent City Band played there on, I think, a Friday night. I can remember asking for a request and talking to the band, but I didn't know them as a musician in those days, I was just another punter.

In about 1955 I was demobbed out of the Army, I had decided that I didn't want to stay in any longer, though it had been a great experience. I had no contacts for musical work so the first thing I did was to join the Musicians Union. The Union in Hull used to run a student orchestra, Sunday mornings at the Windsor Hall, the man in charge was Leslie Rose. Leslie was a pianist and arranger,. He'd had the experience of playing on the liners and was a really good bloke. His Leslie Rose Orchestra played for dancing at the Hull City Hall every Saturday night and needed a third trumpet player. The Orchestra, as far as I can remember consisted of three trumpets, two trombones, five sax's, three or four rhythm a fourteen or fifteen piece outfit. It was quite normal to get a crowd of 1,000 plus in the hall. Apparently the one geezer who had been playing third trumpet wasn't too good, through going to the Student Orchestra I got the job. But of course, you didn't bloody well get paid for it! This is where I think the Union was a bit of a farce because some of the big bands that were playing in those days only paid the key players and all the sitters-in did it for experience. Well perhaps that's a way of learning, I won't go into an argument about that, but if the musicians are playing well they should be paid for it, even if they aren't getting the same rate as the better members of the band. After a few weeks with Leslie Rose I heard of a little band playing Saturday nights at a Church Hall. It was only a six piece with one trumpet, I'd got to know the trumpet player through the Student Orchestra. He wanted to work at the City Hall even though there would be no pay and eventually we swopped jobs. Meanwhile I had met some other guys who were doing small gigs here and there. In those days, none of us had a car. We got one gig at Dairycoates Parish Hall and we all lived in East Hull. Graham Joy was our drummer and he had the unenviable task of getting his kit on and off two buses - we had to change at Hull Bus Station. Naturally the drums got stuck under the stairs and the Conductor was getting a bit agitated, he was due out in thirty seconds, drums off or drums still on. Somehow we dragged them out. The gig we were playing at was a Trawler Skipper's shindig with lots of bottles of 120 proof whisky and it was a really wild party. It was all conducted very well, there was no violence or hooliganism.

By this time I had got a day job working for Imperial Typewriters on Hedon Road. Quite a few of Harry Chatterton's Band worked there and it was through them that I got work with a little band called the Altiners. The line up was piano accordion, piano, drums and a front line instrument. We used to go all over the place doing little country gigs, Brandesburton, Hornsea, Aldbrough. Alan Campy the accordion player had a Jowett Bradford van big enough to carry us and our gear, he lived in Beverley and I lived in Hull, after the gig he would bring me back to Hull for half a crown. We usually got paid about £2 but we always got a good plate of sandwiches and cups of tea. We really played at some out of the way places and of course this might not have a lot to do with jazz, but a lot of the music we played was without dots, played out of the head so I suppose we were improvising in a lot of ways.

After a while of gigging out like this I heard on the grape vine that Tommy Fisher was looking for a second trumpet. His first trumpet was Wally Ingram and his second trumpet had retired. Tommy Fisher's Band was a very well known band in those days, he put out 16 to 18 piece bands at the City Hall and other venues though his regular spot was at the Beverley Road Baths on a Saturday night. I was a bit nervous about it but I rang Tommy. He was a real down to earth fellow was Tommy, he just told me to turn up at their next do and sit in, that would be my audition. I duly sat in, Wally Ingram said I was OK so from that moment I was in the band. I got paid for the audition and that was the difference between Tommy's band and some of the others who liked to put people in and not pay them for playing.

I first met Geoff Woodhouse when he was going around Hull trying to find a venue for a jazz club. Eventually one started at the Windsor Hall on Anlaby Road. It was just a large wooden hut off Argyle Street, there was no licence there so people used to congregate in the Argyle pub before a session and during the interval. There seldom was a real interval, usually one of the local bands would fill, especially if the main attraction was from out of town. I joined the Woodhouse Band when Al Jenner, who had been his trumpet player, went off to go pro. Around that time there were several bands in action, Ted Blackshaw, the 2.19, the Paul Shepherdson Band and there was plenty of work for them all. There was a very late night Jazz Club in the Kevin Ballroom which was over the Fruit Market. This started at 10pm. and went on until the early hours of Sunday morning. It was a place to go on to after you had finished working at a dance, musicians took their instruments along and maybe sat in with the resident jazz band. I played there on one or two occasions, I remember Acker Bilk once came in with some of his band. He'd been playing in Brid. and wanted to play some real jazz. In those days he was probably pressurised to play the popular stuff, but Acker liked to have a drink and play the real stuff. Other visitors to the Club were Mick and Chris Pyne who hailed from Bridlington. Mick was a trumpet player and his brother played trombone, they both play in well known jazz circles in London, Mick is the pianist with the Humphrey Littleton Band. He is and was a natural musician, he sat in with the Woodhouse Band one night at the Windsor Hall playing an alto sax that he'd only had for about a month and he played really well.

Another jazz venue that opened about that time was the Astoria Cinema. That was a real all-nighter, it used to be open from 10pm. to 6am. Many's the time I've played there and stopped a milkman and bought a bottle of milk on the way home. In those days I used to go for a drink in the Corn Exchange. I was in there one night and happened to mention that I was playing at the Astoria that night, they called it the Scene. We were due on at 2am. and I said to Fred Bell, the landlord of the Exchange "I wish I could get a pint of draught Bass to take to the gig because the Astoria is dry" So Fred said "Why don't you take a couple of bottles, I've got some screw top bottles" So I took these along to the Scene with me and when our turn came to play stood them on top of the piano. Well, the bottles he had given me were whisky bottles and the punters were amazed that I was still on my feet after drinking as they thought, two bottles of Scotch!

After a while, I got a different daytime job which entailed travelling and had to drop out of the Woodhouse Band. I worked for Massey-Ferguson the tractor people in Coventry. Geoff Woodhouse had lived in Coventry for some time and he was able to put me in touch with the jazz in that area. There was quite a lot going on in the Midlands. Some of the venues that I remember well were the Pilot at Radcliffe and the Earlsdon Cottage, Saturday nights there was a big band of 14/15 pieces that played at the Mercer's Arms, Fletcher Henderson type music. I got plenty of sit-ins but as I liked to go home on a weekend I turned down the offers to play Friday and Saturday nights.

I did form a little band of my own when I was down there, we played at a pub called the Hollybush in Nuneaton. It was whilst I was in Coventry that I met the famous Wild Bill Davidson.; He was a larger than life character if there ever was one!" John Assell, the drummer from the band that played at the Pilot was woken one morning about 4am. by a loud banging on his door, Wild Bill had been slung out of the Leofric Hotel for causing a bit of a disturbance. I think he'd been ringing for room service in the early hours of the morning and generally being a bit inebriated. We went to see Wild Bill at the Dancing Slipper in Nottingham, Freddie Randall had got a band together including Bruce Turner and Bill. It was a rather informal session, not a concert, I got up to walk past the front of the band and Bill put his hand out and said "Stop, don't walk in front of a player when he's taking a solo". So I said "But I'm just going to the bar to get you a whisky, Bill" He said "Pass, friend". After about three years there I got a job back home and came to Hull to live.

This was when I had a bit of trouble with a lung, so I put the trumpet on top of the wardrobe and forgot all about it for a couple of years. I had also got married and moved to Beverley. During this time a jazz club had re-started at the Blue Bell with Graham Galtrey on clarinet and Trevor Hickson on trumpet, the band was called the Humberside Bluesicians. I didn't go regularly, in fact I only went to see Sandy Brown with the band, I didn't want to be tempted to start playing again. Then the Jazz Club decided to transfer to the Haworth Arms, there was a larger room there and they hoped to tap the student market. The club stayed at the Haworth for a number of years, some landlords encouraged it, others were not too happy. Then John Holborn, otherwise known as Blind Lemon, happened to be short of a trumpet player for his East Coast Jazz Band and it was he who persuaded me to come out of retirement. The first gig I played with Blind Lemon was the Haworth and Champion Jack Dupree was appearing there. It was a full house, about 150 people there. I got through the night all right, though I was very nervous, not having played for two years. A couple of days after that Champion Jack was playing at the University supported by our band and another group called Humber Jug. I played there as well, so gradually got my lip in and we started rehearsals and getting one or two arrangements off. At that time the personnel in the band was myself, Bill Cater on trombone, Blind Lemon on clarinet, Keith Stutt, drums, Harry Ball on bass, Ken Ford, banjo and Joyce Cater on piano.

The Jazz Club was having a lot of success, getting a lot of people in every week and we also used to have out-of-town musicians in to play. People such as Ken Colyer and the Alex Welsh Band. We also had Joe Harriot, he was doing solo tours, he played with just a rhythm section and sat in with the band as well. Joe did several gigs around the area and became friendly with a girl in Hull, so he spent most of his spare time up here. He stayed at the Fox and Coney at South Cave and the landlord used to put on jazz sessions there.

The run at the Haworth was broken when a landlord appeared who was not too happy about having jazz there. Maybe he thought that there was a connection between jazz and drugs and students that was undesirable, whatever, the Club moved to the Spring Street Theatre for a while. After about three months there was another move to the Wolds pub (now the Odd Bottle) and then, on a change of landlords, back to the Haworth.

I must make a mention of a chap from Goole called Ken Storey. He came along to the Haworth one night with a couple of his pals and one of them came along and said "Our mate here plays the tenor sax, can he sit in with the band?" Well, he turned out to be a knockout tenor player. He had had to give up playing 20 years previously when his wife became ill and he had given up playing so that he could look after her. She was the sort of invalid who couldn't walk and he was devoted to her. She died after this long illness and after a while he decided that he would get back into circulation again, so he got his tenor out of the case and started playing once more.

Then I formed a band called the New Dixieland Kings and the line up as far as I can remember was myself, Graham Galtrey, clarinet, Ken Storey, tenor, Harry Chat, trombone, Brian Thompson, drums and Bill Cater on bass. We played at the Jazz Club occasionally and also at Spring Street which had now become known as Hull Arts Centre. One gig we did there was with Bruce Turner, he was very impressed with Ken Storey's playing - his words to me were "He even looks like Lester Young"! and Ken did. Another time Bud Freeman was going to appear at the Arts Centre and I was asked at short notice to put a band together to accompany him. What we call a Scratch Band. I was able to get everyone but a drummer and then Trevor Hickson told me of a young lad called Martin Beadle. He was only 14 but was very good for his age. Bud was going around playing and talking about his life and jazz in general. We started the night off to warm things up a bit and then Bud came on and did his stint. In the paper there was a review of this performance and one the critics mentioned the supporting band and he didn't talk about it in glowing terms! One of the things he said was that the Bandleader kept referring to a scrap of paper in his pocket. Actually it was just to remind me of the numbers that my scratch band could play!

I've never been keen on going to concerts where people sit in rows of seats and listen very quietly to the music. I much prefer the informal Club atmosphere, I don't mind if the audience are talking and drinking when the band is on, it all adds to the atmosphere. On the particular occasion that I'm referring to, at the Hull Arts Centre, Bud Freeman was playing with the rhythm section, it went very flatly indeed and I thought he needs to relax a bit more. I went to the bar and asked what he was drinking, turned out to be Gin and Tonic so I bought a double. The next time there was a pause in the performance I walked on stage and put it on top of the piano. His jaw dropped, he was amazed, he didn't realise that this was going to happen. He mentioned it later on and said Oh, someone came from the audience and gave me a drink and it was much appreciated . When he saw me in the dressing room he said I might have known that that was going to be another musician who'd do that !

During this era, the Jazz Club used to organise Riverboat Shuffles. These took place on Saturday evenings and there would be four or five bands playing. The boat used to sail from the pier about 7.30 - 8pm., cruise up and down the river and get back shortly before midnight. To hire the ferry boat it cost £120, this included the crew, the tickets were 12/6d. each. One complication was that the voltage on board was 110 so that we had to have transformers for the microphones, another difficulty arose one night when the Paul Shepherdson Band was going to play - no piano. The gig had been organised by an agent, not the Hull Jazz Club and they hadn't realised that a piano was needed. This was before the days of the small electronic keyboards. Whatever, on this particular night the usual service boat was waiting for ours to cast off before it could get in, we were scrounging round the nearby pubs to borrow a piano and get it on board, no easy task! On another cruise the Wool City Band from Bradford were playing and hadn't been paid what they expected or something. They were going to throw the piano into the river and as it had been hired from Gough and Davy's we weren't too keen on that happening.

In those days pianos were often a bit of trouble because you might turn up at a gig and the piano would be out of tune, sometimes even a whole tone flat, you just had to manage with it the best you could. Nowadays, of course, with electric pianos this trouble doesn't arise because a band can be self contained with it's own rhythm section.

Other venues that I have played at in the recent past have been the Maybury with Trevor Hickson; I played valve trombone there but I got rid of it after a while when I found that I couldn't get the sound from it that I liked. The Dog and Duck at Walkington was a popular place on a Sunday evening and for a time there was a band at the King Billy in Cottingham on Summer Sunday lunchtimes - al fresco! The King Billy Friday nights continue, they've been going for five or six years and are very popular, good atmosphere in the Old Brewery. Ken Ford still promotes jazz at the Piper Wednesday evenings with local and visiting bands.

I might just say in finishing that learning to play an instrument and playing jazz in particular has really been the best thing I could have done. It's opened up new worlds for me which I could never have seen or experienced if I hadn't done this.

Wilf Moran

In the late 50's and early 60's I was in the R.A.F. I had been taught as a kid, when I was about 10 or 11 to play the piano accordion, and that's why I can't bear an accordion any more! I went to sea when I was about 15 or 16. I had been brought up on classical music, if it wasn't Chopin I didn't want to listen to it. My friend brought a few jazz records to sea with him, a lot of the big band stuff, Count Basie, Bunny Berrigan and I eventually got interested in it and decided that I would buy a trumpet. My friend bought a guitar. I remember the first time we made this decision, in fact it goes back a bit further, we'd been at home on leave and seen a film called 'Young Man of Music' starring Doris Day and the guy with a dimple in his chin, I forget his name just now (Kirk Douglas - Ed.). Harry James was playing the music and I was very impressed with that, I went to see it day after day for about a week. We were in East Africa, in Dar-es-Salaam and we went ashore looking for instruments to buy. Of course we were not able to find anything there, but I remember being taken by a black trumpet player to a club there. I don't suppose he was much of a trumpeter but he did teach me the fingering on the trumpet.

When I got home, in fact you will probably find it in the records of the Hull Daily Mail somewhere, my father put an advert. in the paper saying "Trumpet required, must be cheap". It was cheap, it was 8 quid that I paid for it! It may have been cheap but it was like blowing through a piece of wood. I took it to sea with me, I knew a little bit about music because I'd had sessions, on the piano accordion. I used to go and practice the trumpet on the steering flat where the steering engine was installed, it was like playing in a cathedral. One time I was on a coaster and we were in fog, going up the north east coast, the Captain kept slowing the ship down because he could hear this noise, he thought it was another ship blowing its fog-horn. It was me practising in the steering flat; every time I heard the engine slow down I stopped playing and then the engines would come back again, I'd start playing again and he'd stop the engines, and so it went on.

I got into jazz through this pal of mine and because of that I am influenced by Louis Armstrong, as nearly every trumpet player is, Bunny Berrigan, the big band stuff, the swing band stuff so that when jazz did come along as popular music, the banjo plinking away, the English jazz, the Monty Sunshine music, I just didn't like it at all. It was Bunny Berrigan's 'I Can't Get Started' that got me started because I was very impressed with the way he played the trumpet. What I did in those days was to put a record on and try and play along with it. I just found my way around the music like that. Other people I was concerned with were Bobby Hackett, who played some super stuff with Jack Teagarden. Then I decided that I would join the Air Force. I had a bit of an idea on the trumpet, but not a lot, so I asked if I could join the R.A.F. Band, which was the Central Band of the Royal Air Force. I went off to Uxbridge for an audition. I failed the audition for the band, they told me to practice this and practice that and come back in six weeks time. I thought that was the brush off, which was stupid really. I could have gone into an Army Band which was even dafter, I'd been told that the Army was all bullshit and I didn't want to be cleaning my shoes all the time so I went into the Air Force as a Wireless Operator. While I was in the Air Force I was doing quite a bit of playing with bands that were virtually the same sort of standard as myself. I went to a place near Newcastle, R.A.F. Owston and there was a guy there called Tommy Burton, I saw him about three weeks ago in concert, and he's now considered to be one of the top stride piano players in the country. Tommy was a policeman in the Air Force when I first met him. He was a marvellous piano player and I played with him in the pubs quite a lot. Then I was posted to Cyprus and played with bands there, jazz bands and whatever and I was getting a bit better musically speaking.

When I returned from Cyprus although I was still a Wireless Operator/ Telegraphist I joined the Fighter Command band which was a brass band. That was a marvellous part of my career because I had two years with that outfit. We used to play at all the big hotels in London, the big ones on Park Lane like the Grosvenor, and that was a Hell of an experience. When I was demobbed, I'd got a job in Hammonds and I was playing with a few of the lads, Bill Cater and people like that and of course these are people that probably know more about it than I did. There was a trombone player that we used to play with some-times, he came from York and was a remarkable player despite not being able to read a note of music. We had a duet to play together and when I gave him the dots he didn't even know the position on the slide. He was forming a band to be called the 2.19 Jazz Band with Ches Chesterman on trumpet. Ches is a guy who has really made out in the south as far as jazz is concerned, he does a lot for Radio Two now, or he did when they had the Jazz Club.

I can remember my nephew once coming and asking me how to play, I went down to a youth club but they were totally useless. But after a while it was surprising how they improved.

A place on the go at about that time was the Windsor Hall, I played down there with various bands. There was another place at that time, the Astoria Cinema. They used to have all-night jazz sessions and of course this was really revolutionary stuff. Everybody was worrying about the thought of being raped and of course nothing like that ever happened! But it was all night and I remember I used to take my sisters slimming tablets to keep awake, I didn't realise that they were bennies, but that was what they were!

This was when Paul Shepherdson started the original East Coast Jazz Band, long before Blind Lemon started his East Coast Band. We were looking for a clarinet player and were lucky enough to get Ted Tarling. He was a remarkably good saxophonist and just as able on the clarinet. The funny thing was that according to more academic musicians his fingering was all wrong. But nobody had the cheek to tell him, he was too good! Pity that you never hear him now, it seems that he has just called it a day - like other musicians who were playing around that time.

It was about this time that the bands were beginning to dress up, the fashion was set by outfits like Dick Charlesworth and his City Gents. We, that is Paul's band, were approached by a promoter to do a gig, I forget where it was just now, and the promoter wanted us to dress up like cavemen! Needless to say we didn't like the idea! We did a lot of gigs on the south bank, Grimsby and places like that. Paul fancied himself as a bit of a joker in those days, he still does for that matter, and one of his jolly japes was to pull up alongside a pedestrian and ask for directions in broken English with a heavy German accent. Naturally this had to misfire, he tried it one day and the bloke asked him if he was German. When Paul replied "Ja" he got directions all right, in German, the fellow he'd asked being German.

There was plenty of work to be had in the clubs, particularly for pianists, this was before the electronic organs began to come in, and there were some excellent pianists around. Alan Harmer was one of the very best, but bass players didn't like him, he had such a strong left hand that he could drown them out. Len Hanson is another great pianist, I think he is one of the best jazz players in the county, he plays organ now. We used to go down to the Maybury Hotel on a Monday night, it isn't really a hotel, just a pub, and blow our heads off with Lenny on the piano. Another place I used to play was the New Embassy Club, Tuesday nights. There would be Baz Hewland, Jimmy Marshall (who now lives in Spain) and Brian Milner on piano. Sadly he died young, he was another good piano player. He formed the Milner Marshall Band and later his brother together with Alf Rivetts and Jimmy Marshall were the resident trio at the Westfield Club during its heyday.

I left Hull in 1962 and went to work in London. I managed a few sit-ins but I spent more time listening to the bands down there. When I came back to Hull I played quite a lot at the Haworth Arms, I think that that is one of the best venues in town from the playing point of view, I've always enjoyed my times there.

As this is all about Hull Jazz and Jazzmen I don't think I ought to say too much about my efforts to bring bands in from out of town. The bands were good, the best, but the support for them was poor. I never could understand why people would fill somewhere like the New Theatre to listen to Chris or Acker but wouldn't want to come and see the same bands in a club atmosphere!

It's good to see that there are some talented young musicians coming along into the jazz scene. People like Andy Peacock, Gary Gillyot,

Martin Jones and Paul Sharples. Andy is very versatile, not many know how good he is on piano for instance, he can play anything and well. Martin Jones I remember from the days playing at the Haworth Arms, he'd sit in the front row and just listen and learn, now I think of him as the best trumpet man in town, he's done well out of town as well. Gary, what can I say about Gary? Probably the right word is brilliant, and Paul seems to be a natural jazz man, blowing a sweet sound on the trombone.

That seems to be about all I can manage, I hope it has been of some interest.

Dave Peacock

For me it all started when I was about 14 and attending Hatfield Secondary Modern. Our usual music lessons consisted of singing folk songs and traditional airs, the British Grenadiers, Greensleeves, numbers like that, a fine old teacher, good piano player, but strictly traditional British songs you know! Then one day a student teacher called Haywood came along - he was on teaching practice I think. He had brought a clarinet along and played a bit of jazz, a breath of spring air, then he said "We will have a little concert, I want you all to bring a record, a favourite record". I had a record of Louis singing Basin Street Blues and I took that to be played, there were one or two other jazz records some rock and roll, but nobody in the class of 40 had anything classical as a favourite record.

After leaving school I got a job with a local television company in Doncaster and could afford to go to the concerts that were being played by bands such as Chris Barber's. The jazz was at a pub in Bentley and they were absolutely superb nights. Then I decided to go to College in Hull and soon got involved, but only as a spectator, listening to the guys who are contributing to this book. Ronnie Burnett and musicians like that used to play at the university, the Old Blue Bell, Red Cellar Club and Kingston Rowing Club and I had some super nights there whilst at College. During the summer holidays I worked for a bank in Reading, it was the most boring job I think I've ever had in my life, but I earned enough to buy my first banjo, that would be about 1959-60, it cost me eight quid and in fact I've still got it. It wasn't a particularly good one but I soon learnt three chords, I didn't play in a band, just pottered about.

After finishing College I went to see the world, visited a few countries, saw different Continental Jazz Bands. I was interested in Jazz and went to concerts whenever I could.

I was very busy for a few years and I think it must have been 1975 when I started actually playing with a band. With my wife I used to go to the old 'George' down Walton Street. There was a band there consisting of Dave Mitchell on valve trombone, Trevor Hickson, trumpet, Bob Penwarn, clarinet, Freddie Harrison, bass and on piano sometimes Gordon Finlay and sometimes Alan Harmer. It was a good night out, we used to listen to the music and have a couple of pints. One night I got talking to Bob and Dave and they asked me if I played an instrument and my wife said "Ay, he's got a banjo in the loft". With that people started ringing me up "Get that banjo out". We had a bit of practice, practised to records a lot and after a while they asked me to come down to the Maybury Hotel, that would be 1976.

The first band I sat in with consisted of Harry Chatterton, Trevor Hickson, Bob Penwarn, Alan Harmer, Freddie Harrison and Eric Wright on drums. I used to sit at the back and play and after three weeks or so became part of the band. I well remember one night, something cropped up and the front line stopped playing - I stopped playing - and Eric Wright said to me "You never stop playing, doesn't matter what happens or what you play, you keep playing till it sorts itself out". That has been a good tip.

After that it's quite interesting. In 77/78 there was a group formed called 'Snowy, Bob and Dave', Snowy being Trevor Hickson and we did a club act, did many, many clubs Dixieland. The big problem was the drummer, you couldn't rely on the club drummers to back you properly. Some were excellent but others didn't seem really interested or couldn't get the right rhythm. Anyway Martin Beadle joined the band, though he was only about 14 at the time, from then on it was 'Snowy, Bob, Martin and Dave'. We went round the various clubs with the act and also played at the Jazz Club now and again.

One night I won't forget is the time we played the Sunnyside Club at Cleethorpes. The music was going well, mainly because two of the club musicians backing us, bass and drums, also played in the Apex Jazz Band. Apart from that, I thought it was bloody freezing in there, I was so engrossed in playing my banjo and concentrating on what we were doing that it took me a time to realise. When the compere called out the Bingo prizes he said that so-and-so had won a joint of beef, a frozen joint of beef and they couldn't find it. To cut a long story short I'd been sitting on the bloody thing all night! Clubland was hard work but enjoyable and I learned a lot about music, well, not so much about music but a lot about clubland. When Bob dropped out of the group Trevor Hardy came in for a while but the bookings sort of petered out.

After that we went to Scarborough a couple of times and sat in with a band that played the 'The Barn'. One night a chap turned up, check shirt and covered in muck and sat down at the drums. We started playing, the place was packed and I suddenly thought it was ever so easy to play - what it was was this drummer was so good you couldn't hear him until he stopped playing. I said to this guy "Oh, you've done a bit" and he told me he didn't get the chance to play often, only every six or eight weeks. He was a farmer now but he had had fifteen years as drummer with the John Barry Seven.

My next long time band was Johnnie Holborn's East Coast Jazzmen. Ken Ford had decided to move on to do other things and I took his place. That was a very good line up. Johnnie on clarinet, Dave Mitch on trumpet, Bill Cater, Ernie Price on bass and Pete Robby on drums. I learnt a lot from that band, played different numbers with a lot of Kenny Ball stuff. It was all slightly commercial but it was nice to play New Orleans style. A very good audience in those days at the Haworth Arms, it was packed every Tuesday. There were some super times and John must have run that band for years and years.

I have been lucky enough to get a lot of help and information from Joyce Cater. I think she must have written all the chord books for everybody in town. It doesn't matter whose chord book you look at, the trail always leads back to Joyce. If you get stuck with a number all you need to do is call her up and she'll ring back in two minutes and say "Yes, those three chords, I've worked them out" and that was it, she is always dead right, a lot of credit to Joyce. She is ever helpful to all musicians.

Colin McGarrigal was the Headmaster of a private school in Scarborough and quite an enthusiastic jazz drummer. He formed a band and I was asked to join, we did a lot of jobs for the school and also 'Society' jobs. The two Trevors, Hickson and Hardy were in the front line, Fred Percival was on bass and Mike Gordon on piano. I remember doing one gig in Sloane Square, London, we doubled with a belly dancer and a fire eater, quite a night! We worked a lot of stately homes with that band, Colin had contacts everywhere. The band ran on for some time but gradually faded away when Colin moved to York.

Around that time I had a night at the City Hall that was pretty amazing. The Hull Philharmonic was playing and Geoffrey Heald-Smith was in charge. He was a fine musician and gifted with perfect pitch. We had all come in evening dress, bow ties, and halfway through the classical concert he turned off the orchestra, we took over. The line up there

90

was Heald-Smith on piano, Trevor Hardy clarinet, Harry Chatterton, trombone, Martin Beadle, drums and Janet Heald-Smith on bass. The audience thought we were marvellous, we trooped off to great applause after about half an hour and the classical concert re-started.

That takes us up towards the 80's and I was still playing with the East Coast Jazzmen. I sometimes played with the Trevor Hickson Band but then I went off to the Pacific for three months. Had good night at the Jazz Club before I went! I was stationed in the Solomon Islands and to say there was not much to do would be an understatement. We were 28 miles from the nearest shop. At least we had a good radio and were able to pick up broadcasts from Australia, we used to enjoy the Peter Charles Jazz programme which was on for three hours every night. Mainly Australian jazz

More memories of playing for the River Boat Shuffles, playing in pubs and clubs (one night at Golcar the power failed and they were amazed that it didn't stop us playing) even in the open air. Then one night, coming home from the Haworth Arms, Bill Cater told me that the landlord at the King Billy in Cotty wanted a band to play on Friday nights - the jazz there has been on for nearly 6 years without a break. Lately we have been varying the bands although the Storyville and J. J. Jazzband play most of the nights, but we have had some very good times there, good atmosphere, swinging place.

Really though my main hobby is still sailing, at various times I disappear across to Holland and listen to (and sometimes sit in with) the bands there. I'm just an enthusiastic amateur who enjoys playing jazz, playing with a jazz band. We keep pottering on at the King Billy. I hope that's enough for you Laurie!

Paul Shepherdson

I suppose the over riding factor in anything I have ever done has been the need to entertain and I have been very fortunate in not only being able to play jazz but also to be involved in musical theatre and other forms of drama. I actually started in about 1957 and along with thousands of youngsters at that time formed a skiffle group within the confines of the church youth club. This was known as the Sioux City Seven a name which people found great difficulty in getting used to but which we stuck with. It wasn't a very good group, we failed an audition of Opportunity Knocks after spending a lot of money going to Leeds. But one of the important things with the group is that we had discovered in a talent contest at the Regal Cinema, as it was known in those days, one Kay Brewer, Kay came second to our first in the contest. Kay went on to join the Geoff Woodhouse Jazz Band and from there joined the Alan Hirst Dance Band, who were at that time appearing at the Majestic Ballroom in Witham. Kay eventually became known as Kay Garner and became a top sessions singer in London. It was through the skiffle days that I met one John Silcock who is an ardent, ever faithful New Orleans fan, and it was he who founded a jazz club on a Friday night at St. Mary's Church Hall in Cottingham. I was reluctantly dragged down there one night and from that moment I was hooked. If I remember, some of the musicians that were playing at the time were Ches Chesterman on trumpet, Glen Gibb on trombone and Brian 'Drag' Kirby on double bass. I believe 'Guts' Grunhill was on drums, but I'm not 100% sure I think that the venue was operated then by Frank Courtney. This jazz club went on for some time and I first met people like Ronnie Burnett. The next band to be formed was, if I remember correctly the Unity Jazz Band and this was based at the Hull College of Art. I myself had just left the College of Commerce.I went along to listen to the band when they played at the Blue Bell pub in Lowgate. Again, I think, on Friday nights. This was a very exciting band and they were emulating the very popular Acker Bilk, dressing in black waistcoats, little curled collars, red ties and pin-stripe trousers that they had found by searching the second- hand shops. I only listened to the band originally because the drummer at the time was Brian Thompson who was awaiting call-up. Brian eventually went, they asked me to take over the drum seat, and I had about 18 very happy months with the Unity Band. An exciting band with musicians such as Ron Burnett on trombone, Tony Dugdale on clarinet, Alan Peacock on trumpet and Ricky Tanton on banjo. We used to do the College dances, I can remember playing at the Art College for the Ugly Bug Ball. That band continued for some time and with the boys at the time leaving the Art College, Tony Dugdale who was really running the band left and he asked me to take the band over as he thought I was putting in more time on it than anyone else. This was true and partly because I didn't have a proper job at the time. We kept the band going for some time, but like all these things people drift away and round about the same time I was asked to join the Geoff Woodhouse band. Interestingly enough there was a drummer with the Geoff Woodhouse outfit called Mike Heap. Mike, I believe, had decided to go into the Working Men's Clubs to earn some money, leaving the drum seat free. The Woodhouse band was exceptional, it had Al Jenner on trumpet. Unfortunately Geoff and I had to part company because I was still running my own band and dates tended to clash. Ronnie Burnett on trombone and various members in the rhythm section, Noel Flint I remember and of course Mick Pyne who sometimes had Chris with him and both of whom have gone on to fame and fortune. Unfortunately Geoff and I had to part company because every time I was offered a job I took it for my band and Geoff thought I ought to give it to his band, so it obviously wasn't going to work. This introduced to the Woodhouse band a drummer called Ronnie Dunn, who I thought was very good indeed. Very modern, and he was the only drummer I ever came across who tilted his snare drum towards him. This was quite unusual and whenever I sat in it was impossible to play. Nonetheless he was an excellent drummer and I believe he went off to turn professional and work on the boats. This was actually after Kay Garner had left the Woodhouse Band and gone on to pastures new. Just to go back for a moment to the Unity Jazz Band, the clarinettist that took over from Tony Dugdale was Ted Tarling with whom I am fortunately still friendly and Ted was a very fine musician indeed. He was not necessarily sympathetic to the New Orleans Style but played it with fortitude, especially if money was involved! The money was quite insignificant in those days, we would play five hour gigs for what was the equivalent of one pound ten shillings and as much beer as we could drink. A story which I can remember, though unfortunately I wasn't at the gig. The Unity Jazz Band were playing for the birthday party of a gentleman in Malton, I won't mention any names, but he was quite a big noise up there, and of course the party was being held in the grounds of this very large house. In those days, the trumpet player was the only one of us with a driving licence and the Unity Band had managed to acquire the use of a horse-box to take them to this gig, which was quite a long way, the roads in general were pretty awful. They eventually got there and started to play. There was plenty of free drink, which the band imbibed liberally and soon it seemed as if he was in no condition any more. He eventually collapsed and they stopped him playing by pouring punch down his trumpet. He was fairly well unconscious at this time. When it came to driving home, as he was the only one who could drive there was the question of bringing him round and reviving him in general. He insisted on driving, there was not a lot that anyone else could do about it. They duly piled into the horse box and Alan responded by driving through the prize orchard. There was no more work round Malton for them!

He must have recovered from those dizzy days because he is now a highly respected professional man. Various things were available for performers in those days and one of the outstanding things was the opening of Hull's first purpose built, or purpose altered ballroom, which was above the Market Hall in the centre of the Old Town. This was opened by one Roy Tilley and Roy brought the first full-time professional dance band with people like Pete Boston on drums. I remember him particularly well because I went to take some lessons from him. This was a very exciting band but the ballroom did not have sufficient capacity to keep it going and the professionals left. Roy then took in local musicians of which I was one. One of my other duties was as a disc jockey and being a young buck at the time I was quite proud of my gold lame jacket and grey Italian style pointed shoes, in which I walked down Whitefriargate on Thursdays. People must have thought I was mad! It was useful experience however because one or two incidents at the place made me realise that I would never make a disc jockey. Roy was also very keen on jazz and he did employ, on Tuesday nights, musicians to play jazz. He tried all sorts of things like Afro-Cuban jazz, modern jazz, which went reasonably well and he was also a bit of an innovator in that he would have the bands playing in the middle of the dance floor instead of just on the stage. In those days places like this were not licensed and he couldn't serve anything other than soft drinks and sandwiches.

From then I went on and Geoff Woodhouse and myself were instrumental in setting up the first all-night jazz club in Hull, at the Kevin Ballroom. This would start, late on a Saturday night at 11 o'clock when all the musicians had finished their various gigs and they would all congregate at the Kevin. This went on for some time, unfortunately we turned up one night to find that our kit had all been impounded by the bailiff - the bills hadn't been paid.

So that was the end of another era. Another reason for the decline of the Kevin Ballroom was the opening of the Locarno with the now infamous Ivor Kirchin Band, infamous because many of the band members who came to Hull for the first time in their lives, remained, married local girls and still live in Hull.

Norman Barron and George Woodcock are just two and of course the famous Donny Keith. In about 1959, the jazz club that had been operating at St. Mary's Church Hall, also known as the Vestry Rooms, Cottingham, moved to the now famous Windsor Hall on Argyle Street. This was a glorified hut, that's the best way to describe it, there was no bar of course, but the Argyle pub, was on the opposite side of Anlaby Road and that was made good use of by musicians, girl friends and everyone else concerned. The Windsor Hall was a very exciting venue and very popular locally because all the big name bands of the time appeared there. Not just Kenny Ball and Acker Bilk, Chris Barber and people like that, but also lesser known bands like Mick Mulligan, who had of course George Melly singing with him. My favourite band of the time was the Bruce Turner Jump Band. The Alex Welsh band also appeared there. It was at this time that I met the Mike Peters Florida Jazz band. The rest is history!

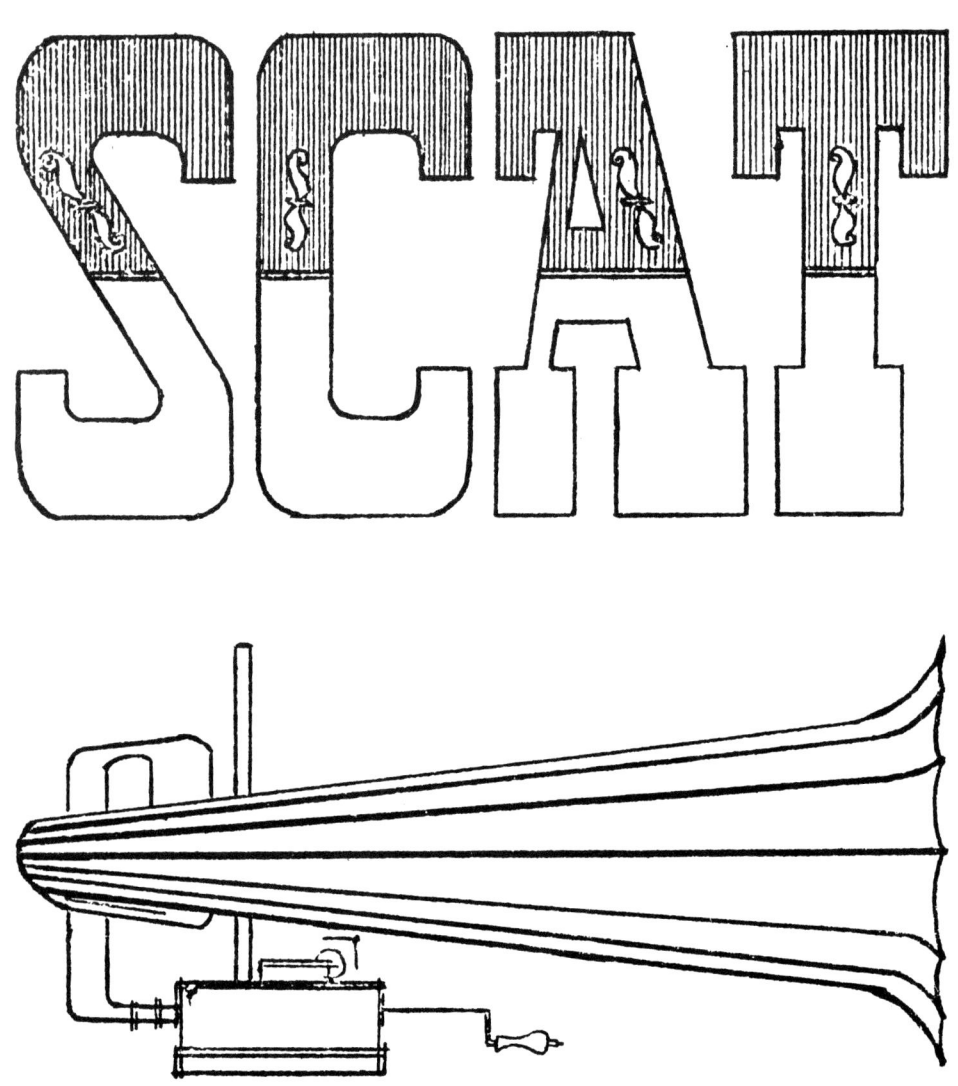

SCAT

MAGAZINE OF THE COTTINGHAM RHYTHM SOCIETY

TWO PENCE

"JAZZING AROUND" by Avo Avison of the Bob Wallis Band.

As you no doubt know, it all started in Bridlington a few years back. Bob (Wallis) and I were friends, and his mother let us use a room up in the attic of their house. We decorated it, installed a gram and started building up a record collection. We built up quite a collection in time and were very proud of it. Of course we weren't satisfied just to listen to jazz, and soon we wanted to play it.

We both belonged to the same brass band and we both played cornet. It was decided that I would have to take up the trombone for playing jazz, but I couldn't afford one just then, so we persuaded another pal of ours to join the brass band on trombone then I could borrow his instrument for playing jazz.

We started looking round for people to form a band with us and heard about a marvellous clarinettist who was living in Bridlington, so Bob and I went to visit him. We were really impressed by his record collection and eventually persuaded him to get his instrument and be auditioned. All he could play was "Trouble in Mind" very slowly, but we were really impressed. That's how Tony Grunhill joined the band. Eventually Cyril Stork joined us on clarinet so Tony took up the drums.

We started playing the Blue Bell in Hull, there was a packed and enthusiastic audience every week, but then National Service caught up with me in 1951 and I was called up into the Army and posted to Egypt. Alan 'Drool' Walker took my place in the band.

After I got demobbed, Bob moved down to London and I followed him. Acker Bilk was the first band I played with down there. He had just come up from Bristol and turned professional. I stayed with him for about four months before he gave me the sack! Well, Johnny

Mortimer was available and I wasn't very good. I could only play about five notes on the trombone then.

The next job I had was with Pete Deucher. He was forming a band to take out to Germany. What a shambles that turned out to be! The first time the whole band met each other was on the boat going over. The only other member of the band I knew was the clarinettist who I had met by accident in a pub a couple of nights before.

That trip was doomed from the start, we had a coloured drummer with us who was quite good, but on the first night at the club the management said he would have to go or we would all have to. For the rest of the stay we had to use various German drummers.

It was a shocking band - I know I was bad - but I was no worse than the others. Chris Bateson was on trumpet and as he hadn't been playing long he didn't know many tunes. We had to play very long sessions as well, so we were drinking a lot to keep ourselves going. It got to the stage were we were slipping off for a pint between each number.

It couldn't go on like that of course, and after about a month the chap who ran the place came and told us we would have to go as we were the worst band they had ever had there. The trouble, or one of the troubles, was that we got so drunk! There was a post on the side of the stage and I used to have to put my arm around it and hold myself up whilst I was playing.

Anyway, we came back to England and Deucher decided to form another band. He kept me on trombone and Dave Saxley on clarinet and a bloke from Manchester, Bill Robinson, joined us on trumpet. Also he got a complete new rhythm section.

A month later I got married in Bridlington and the following day I went back to Germany and stayed there for eleven months! We did a big tour round Hamburg, Duisburg, Dusseldorf, Wuppertal and down the Rhine Valley. It was marvellous, I really enjoyed it, and this band was all right as well.

We decided to come home the following January and the band more or less broke up. I 'retired', went back to Bridlington and took a job as an electrician (that's my trade).

I had one last fling on the night I arrived back in England. I met Acker Bilk and he invited me to go to Dartford with them and have a blow with the band. I sat in with them for two or three numbers and had a marvellous time, then I dashed over to Gravesend, which wasn't too far, to see Bob, who was playing there. I sat in with them and enjoyed it - I blew my head off nearly.

Next day I went north with the intention of giving up music. About the only occasions I played whilst I was back in Bridlington were when I depped for Glen Gibb in the 2.19 Band. I stuck it for about three months, but I wasn't happy and Bob kept asking me to join the band. Anyway, in the end he offered me a good job and found us somewhere to live, so I went south again and joined the Storyville Jazzmen.

I'm happy playing with band and I like the music we play. I would like to progress, but at the moment I'm playing to the extent of my technique. I want to be a musician, but obviously I'm not a musician just playing jazz. I don't want to lose the feeling for jazz, but I do want to be an all-round musician.

My tastes in jazz are varied. I like it all really. I like a lot of modern and a lot of trad. The Lewis Band is a long way removed from the Ellington

Band, but I like them both. My favourite trombonist is Trummy Young. I used to like Ory and Robinson a lot, and I still do, but I think Trummy Young combines the best of them both.

I don't think I am influenced by anyone, I never have enough time to listen to anyone to be influenced - I haven't got the records anyway. In the early days Robinson and Ory influenced me a lot, but now it should be pure Avison.

Everyone these days seems to have a moan about the jazz scene. I have no real cribs. The only thing that does upset me, though not very much, is that I think the scene in England has gone a bit sour because it's a bit too much commercialised and has too much 'English Influence'. I'm not blaming Chris or Acker for this mind you, but the British bands haven't got the 'earthy' sound they used to have. They're not getting the feeling they should. Otherwise I'm quite happy about everything.

Reproduced from 'SCAT' the magazine of the Cottingham Rhythm Society and later, the Hull Jazz Club. Circa 1962.

Reproduced by kind permission of the then Editor, Frank Courtney:

Copyright F. Courtney 1962.

The Bay City Jazz Band by G. Woodhouse.

As with most bands, the origins of the Bay City are obscure. Under the name Delta Jazzband/Jazzmen the group was active in the Bridlington area during 1957, attaining the dizzy heights of a TV audition. Unfortunately the search that night was for skiffle groups, so Humph was assured of his TV spot for a while longer.

During this early period the personnel hinged around three people, Mick and Chris Pyne playing trumpet and trombone respectively and

Ron Dunn on the drums. Another mainstay joined the band in early 1957, pianist Gerry Rollinson. Recording the comings and goings of the other musicians would read like an extract from the Jazz Directory dealing with some obscure mid 30's studio orchestra - banjos, clarinets and guitars in and out like yo-yos.

Around the turn of last year, however, stability set in with the advent of clarinettist Graham Galtrey and a change of name to the Bay City Jazz Band. With a regular weekly engagement at the 'Galleon Cafe' in Bridlington and sessions at Reighton Hall and Scalby Manor together with jobs in Hull the band's New Orleans style took on a degree of musical polish. However, June was to provide yet another change of personnel with the departure of Graham Galtrey. Having been on the musician's dole since the Al Jenner Band disbanded for the summer, I took over the clarinet chair.

The summer proved a good chance for the band to get to know each other, we had two regular engagements in Bridlington and made several appearances in the North Riding. For that winter though, the decision was made to put the band on a more organised footing. A regular guitarist, Barry Monahan was added and the desired rhythm section completed by '2.19' bassist Denis Aylwyn. In one of the moments of weakness to which jazzmen are prone, the band gave the leadership to me and, as far as is known are still looking for the fruits of this rashness!

Not that the band are being underworked. Regular bookings at Cottingham, appearances each Tuesday at the Kevin Ballroom and, more recently the opening of their own club at the Grovehill Hotel in Beverley each Wednesday, ensure that if not of professional status at least they get regular beer money.

What style are they aiming for? How often that question is asked, and how often they wish they had a straight answer. The truth is, I suppose, no stereotyped style at all. Influenced they certainly are, in sound and style, by groups as varied as Armstrong's All Stars, the Ellington Orchestra and the Eddie Condon mob. Personally I don't think that the label matters in the least, they play in the way that gives them most pleasure and leave it at that.

Since this article was written the band has gone through another change. Pianist Gerry Rollinson has left. Mike Pyne has moved on to the piano and Al Jenner now looks after the trumpet chores. The band now play at Goole Jazz Club every Thursday.

Re-printed from SCAT (by kind permission of Frank Courtney) Spring issue 1959

Jazz Clubs are mushrooming up all over the district these days. In some ways it is a good thing. Never has the public of Hull had it so good! At the same time there is the possibility that they are getting too much of a good thing and will get fed up with jazz — I hope not! The long established "2-19" sessions still take place at the Abercrombie Hotel every Thursday and recently some group whom we have not yet heard, and the name of which we can't discover, started Wednesday sessions at the Ship Inn. Also, we now discover that a jazz club has opened down De Grey Street somewhere, this also meets on a Wednesday. Geof Woodhouse tells me that the Wednesday sessions of the Grovehill Jazz Club at Beverley are not getting much support and that the band now treat it as a practice night. The Kevin Ballroom presents Jazz every Tuesday and a jazz band can be heard at the University Saturday Dance. The Tivoli Jazz Band can be heard blowing at the Tivoli Tavern on a Tuesday. Nothing happens on a Monday night, and the 7-11 Club meet on a Sunday afternoon. That leaves the night with which we are concerned — Friday. We now have direct competition from the Unity Jazz Club and the Club 7-11. The effect of these two clubs opening on the same night as us has shown on our attendances, but not as much as we expected. We recently decided to take a look at our competition and dropped in to their sessions. The Unity meet in the Blue Bell, the stamping ground of many local Jazz Bands at one time or another. The appeal here is for people who like to drink and listen, no room for dancing. As they have no overheads they don't have to worry about charging much — I begrudge them Friday — this isn't fair competition!! The "7-11" is somewhat different; here the Club, like ours, is "dry". There is room for dancing and they make a fair charge for admission. Good straight competition!! We noticed here that they have cribbed our idea of using record covers for decoration, and the hot dog line. The music here is Modern only. As a result of this we have decided that it is rather pointless us carrying on with our public spirited idea of presenting all types of jazz. In future we will devote our Friday evening mainly to "trad" forms of jazz. It is therefore highly unlikely that the wailing sounds of the Freda-Maud Rhythm Aces, the Shemph Wood Quartet or any other modern group, will echo among rafters again — on a Friday anyway'

HULL JAZZ CLUB WINDSOR HALL.

Future attractions include:

July 29th   Bob Wallis & Storyville Jazzmen : Geof Woodhouse Ensemble

Aug. 5th   The Burgundy Jazz Band : Mike Pyne Quartet

Aug. 12th   Pete Deuchar's Ragtime Band : The Burgundy Jazz Band

Aug. 19th   The Burgundy Jazz Band : Mike Pyne Quartet

Aug. 26th   Bruce Turner Jazz Band : Geof Woodhouse Ensemble

Sept. 2nd   Geof Woodhouse Jazz Band : Burgundy Jazz Band

Sept. 9th   Mick Mulligan Jazz Band with George Melly : Geof Woodhouse Ensemble

Sept. 16th   Geof Woodhouse Jazz Band : Burgundy Jazz Band

Sept. 23rd   Mike Peters Jazzmen : Geof Woodhouse Ensemble

<u>EXTRA - DISJOINTED JOTTINGS</u>

By: Paul Shephersdon

The main development so far this season, forgetting for a moment the Kingston Jazzmen, is the fact that an amazing number of new faces have suddenly appeared on the scene. From whence, no one seems to know. They have appeared like flies out of whatever they come out of, and most of them have already settled on the piece of savoury music which most appeals to them.

We at the Bluebell (every Thursday, 6d.) have gathered to our bosom a fair number of these, many of them first year students at the various educational emporiums strewn around our "fair fishing village" to quote a girl friend of one of the London Jazz Bands, so frequently up here these days. This is a vast improvement on last year when the University, to name but one, seemed most uninterested in the 'local lads'!

At last, the upheaval of early September seems to be sorting itself out. The biggest disappointment to many of us was the end of the 2-19 and Unity Jazz Bands, both of them playing a large part in the scene of the past two years. However, these have now been replaced, ("None of us are indispensable", A. E. Newman 1959) and everything is almost back to normal.

Vast internal staff changes have been successfully overcome in the Woodhouse organization, and Geof's new band should be quite something. It's certainly good to have Harry Chatterton on the scene. To quote the trombonist with the Mike Taylor Jazz Band, "They just don't have trombonists like that in provincial bands! What can you do when you have to follow anyone like that?"

I have only one criticism to make. We seem to be getting a number of people of both makes of the (if you'll pardon the expression) "rock and roll" element. The Bluebell is no exception. Providing they are controlled, I have no objection, but don't let us have a repeat performance of the "Anlaby Incident".

The Hull Jazz Colony have quite a good selection of clubs to attend. Sundays, the University. Somewhat marred by Union Passes and Red Tape, but otherwise very good. The Red Cellar Club is now open on Sunday, and it features the Beaver City Band. The Birdland Club, within the precincts of the Kevin Ballroom, opens each Sunday with the Kingston Jazzmen, and I understand that the Majestic Ballroom is changing its Sunday ballroom dancing policy to jazz and pop music. It's also bath night for many of the un-beatnick clan amongst us, so that takes care of that.

On Mondays - nothing. This enables the ravers to prepare for Tuesdays when the Red Cellar Club is open again, this time to the sweet strains of the Kingston Jazzmen. Wednesdays give us the Burgundy Jazz Band at the Bluebell, and the Kingston lot play there on Thursdays. The climax of the week is reached on Fridays when we all gather under the auspices of the Argyle Hotel, where we accumulate sustenance to attend the Hull Jazz Club.

All this we already know, but what would you write about with a fortnight's notice ....

HOME GROWN

Hull and surrounding districts have managed to produce some quite notable jazzmen, some of them having found national fame, others preferring to stay on "home ground".

The name that currently springs to mind in this respect is Bob Wallis. Bob was born in Bridlington, but Hull was the scene of his early success in the jazz world, as he led his band weekly at the Bluebell and wherever else he could find work. After overcoming a bout of ill-health, Bob is now established as the leader of one of this country's leading bands. Two members of Bob's present band also hail from this area - Avo Avison, his trombonist is also from Bridlington and played in Bob's first Hull based band, and Brian "Drag" Kirby, a Hull lad who before heading south to join Bob's Storyville Jazzmen, played Bass with the Crescent City and Unity Bands.

A "local lad" who has found fame not only in the jazz field, but also in the entertainment world generally, is Kenny Baker. Kenny was born and brought up at Withernsea, but travelled the few miles to Hull to start carving himself a career in the music business, and very successfully he managed it too!!

Al Jenner, who had practically become Hull's "grand old man" of jazz (has he worked out how old he is yet?) has recently joined the Eggy Ley Jazzmen for a tour of Germany. Al has been on the local scene for many years now, in fact to some of us Al is the local scene, and I'm sure things in this City won't be the same without him.

Bridlington has produced more than its fair share of worthwhile jazzmen (it must be the sea air!) Besides Bob Wallis and Avo Avison, there are the Brothers Pyne. Mick, still undecided whether to concentrate on piano or trumpet, and Chris, at present wearing a uniform of R.A.F. blue, who's trombone playing has been sadly missed of late.

The drumming of Ron Dunne was first heard in Bridlington and can now be heard at the Kevin Ballroom, where he appears with the Roy Tilley Band or with the Jazz Diplomats.

Another Bridlington native is Gerry Rollinson, one time pianist with the Bay City Jazz Band and currently playing Vibes with the Teddy Barker Group.

Teddy Barker leads his group at The New York Hotel - they must be one of the few bands playing for dancing that can get away with playing jazz most of the time. Because he is hidden away at the Hotel most of the time Teddy's work is not heard much on the local jazz scene, but I can assure you he is a first class jazz pianist. His work as a writer and arranger is also worthy of note, and I hear that a composition of his has been accepted for use as background music for a film.

And for those of you who are not really interested in jazz - David Whitfield is a "local lad" to be proud of!!

107

FOUR BAR CODA

By Geof Woodhouse

The Grand Old Man of the Hull Jazz Scene, the man who
nourished those early glimmers of jazz interest stirring inside
Tony Grunnill, Al Jenner, Bob Wallis, Col Lilley, Drag Kirby and
several others (including myself), the man who did more for jazz
in Hull in the "dark days" than anyone - yet I doubt if more than
a handful of people recognise him when he pays one of his infre-
quent visits to a local club.

The Jim Stork school for budding jazzmen I suppose we could
name it in retrospect, that sedate Sunday afternoon gathering in
Balta House on Beverley Road. Your shilling entitled you to a
couple of hours of recorded jazz; a cup of tea and a biscuit;
perhaps a lecture from Tony Grunnill about King Oliver; perhaps
a discussion on the rival virtues of Johnny Dodds and Sidney Bechet
and always a selection of Jim's latest "unobtainables" from America.

Don't get me wrong, this wasn't in the middle of the war, this
was a modest eight years ago, but to the record collector of today
with a vast array of discs from which to choose, the situation
then was unimaginably bleak and in those circumstances a record
collection of the magnitude and scope of Jim Stork's was a veritable
Utopia.

These recollections are prompted by the recent re-appearance
on the local scene of numerous Old Boys of Stork College.   Bob
Wallis and Drag Kirby are, of course, fairly regular performers at
the Windsor Hall and Don Kennington, one time tuba/alto sax/clari-
net with the erstwhile Port of Hull Jazz Band made the pilgrimage
from Bletchley to be on the Club's recent Riverboat Shuffle.

Don and I were discussing the various styles that have been
distilled out of the violently traditional old school, and the
instruments to which people eventually settled.   Visualise if you
will Tony Grunnill on clarinet, Al Jenner on banjo and Col Lilley
on trombone - it all really happened!   Can't say I ever got close
enough to Tony to hear his clarinet playing and I never was sufficient of a judge of banjo playing to pass comment on the 1952
Jenner, but this much I can say - Col Lilley could be numbered
amongst the five worst trombonists this world has ever known!

Perhaps Jim Stork sometimes has reason to reflect on those
of his flock who have gone astray.   On a recent visit to the Club
when my circus were the noise providers, his companion John
Collinson (old Stork Collegian, sometime pianist) wasted absolutely
no time whatever getting Jim and himself out of earshot of our
decidedly non-Jelly Roll, non-Oliver, non-Lewis outpourings.

Now for this year's controversy.   Under the heading of "Jazz
Jottings" in the Hull and Yorkshire Times the other weekend,
feature writer John Rodgers gave prominence to an experiment
carried out in connection with the recently disputed origins of
jazz.   The details of the experiment I shan't bother to recite
(you should read "Jazz Jottings" anyhow, it's written for you!)but

THE 2-19 JASS BAND

The 2-19 Jass Band, which is now the Society's resident group, was originally formed by members of the Hull College of Art to take part in a Students' Rag Procession some years ago. After several months of steady practice at the College, the Band felt it was time to extend their activities and they opened their own Jazz Club at the Blue Bell Hotel, Market Place, Hull.

They held sway there for over eighteen months and built up quite a large following for their branch of Jazz. Their aims have changed very little during the time they have been formed, they still try to play authentic sounding New Orleans Style Jazz, but are attempting to get their own individual sound by taking influences from all good New Orleans Jazz, rather than copying any one group of musicians.

The origin of the Band's name often has many people guessing - in actual fact it is derived from an old New Orleans Blues, the 2-19 Blues, which refers to the departure time of a Crescent City Train. The Band recently adopted the "gimmick" JASS, this being the way the word was spelt when it originated in Chicago in the early days.

The Band's popularity is increasing in the Hull area, and while in London on a playing-holiday they found that their brand of jazz was just as acceptable to Southern ears. They received offers of several return engagements which they hope to fulfil in November. They also hope to record for one of the London specialist jazz labels.

The present line up includes only two "founder members", Clarinetist/Leader Keith "Shunt" Smith and Trombonist Glen Gibb. Glen is still a student at the College of Art and Keith is at present working in an Architects Office. The front line is completed by youngest member of the Band, Graham "Chez" Chesterman. Chez who works in the office of a local Paint Manufacturers, is one of the most promising of the local jazz musicians, with a fiery cornet style reminiscent of the early playing of Louis Armstrong.

The rhythm section consists of Ken Ford on Banjo, Dennis Aylwin on Bass and Tony "Guts" Grunnill on Drums. Ken, who works for an Engineering Firm, joined the Band about eighteen months ago, and his playing has improved tremendously in this time. Tony is employed in the Hull Office of a well-known Brewery and has been connected with the local jazz scene for many years. He was with Hull's first jazz band, The Bob Wallis Jazz Band, and joined the "2-19" about a year ago, when the group he was then with, The East Coast Stompers, broke up. Dennis started playing the Bass only a short time ago, but is quickly mastering the instrument and finding himself in great demand. Besides playing with the "2-19" he also handles the bass chores with the Bay City Jazz Band and various small groups. He is equally adept on Tuba (he played this instrument with the Band when he recently broke his Bass) and Trombone, but his Trombone playing is these days limited to Police Band work.

There they are, six people from different walks of life, but with one common interest - the playing of good jazz!

T.G.

•————————•

109

0: **DISP JAZZHIST DTA.** By courtesy of Ken Ford.

1950	Bob Wallis formed Band.
1950	Port of Hull (jazz band) existed.
1954	Bob Wallis went to London.
25/11/56	Humphrey Littleton Band at City Hall, Bruce Turner, Jim Bray, Eddie Taylor, John Pickard, Johnnie Parker, Fred Legon.
20/12/56	Chris Barber's Jazz Band, City Hall.
1957	University Jazz Band. Paul Shepherdson formed band, Bill Newman.
1957	Unity Jazz Band, Unity Jazz Club Saturday sessions a St. John's Newland Parish Hall, 1/- to join, 2/6 admission.
1957	2.19, Ken Ford joined band.
23/1/57	Eddie Condon and his Jazz All Stars, plus Humphrey Littleton and his Band, admission 6/6 (stalls).
13/2/58	Half term dance, College of Art, Ticket 2/6, Unity, 2.19, Bay City Jazz Bands, Pilgrims Skiffle Group.
1958	2.19 went to London, played Wood Green Jazz Club, had crash in Mini-bus.
1958	2.19, all, joined Musicians Union for London trip.
1958	Folk Song to Jazz Concert at Bevin House.
1959	Windsor Hall sessions started under auspices of Cottingham Rhythm Society.
1959	Crescent City Jazz Club existed.
17/7/59	Bob Wallis and his Storyville Jazzmen, Cottingham Rhythm Society, Vestry Rooms, Cott. also 2.19 Jass Band, 4/-
21/8/59	Bob Wallis Storyville Jazzmen, Cottingham Rhythm Society, Vestry Rooms,2.19. Jassband, (return visit) 4/- admission.
1959	2.19 left Abercrombie (Winter).
1960	Burgundy Jazz Band formed by Ken Ford and Guts Grunhill.
1960	2.19 disbanded.
1960	Burgundy Jazz Band, open air gig at East Park.
11/6/60	Riverboat Shuffle with Alex Welsh Band, 2.19 Jass Band, Mike Pyne Trio, Unity Jazz Band, Maryland Band, 10/-, Cottingham Rhythm Society.

10/6/61	Jazz Cruise by Cott. Rhythm Society and K upon Hull Arts Festival, Bob Wallis and his Storyville Jazzmen, Alex Welsh Band, Geoff Woodhouse Band, Unity JB, Mike Taylor JM. 10/6.
1961	Concert at Windsor Hall, University Band, Burgundy Band, Geoff Woodhouse Band, Unity JB.
1962	Trad Band contest.
,5/62	Riverboat Shuffle 10/6, Blackshaw Band.
10/9/62	Paul Shepherson's Jazzmen, opening of Ritzmond Jazz Club at Eureka Cinema, Hessle Road, free for members of old Matador Jazz Club.
1966	Trevor Hickson started jazz sessions at Adelaide Club.
1966	Humberside Bluesicians formed.
1967	East Coast Jazzmen, Blind Lemon formed Band.
1969	East Coast Jazzmen won Hull Parks Dept. Talent Contest. Frowned on by Hull Variety Artistes Assn. (They were members) Not the done thing.
1969	Riverboat Shuffle, special feature front page Hull and Yorks. Times.
1969	Midrode Quintet, re-formed band playing at Blue Bell.
6/3/70	Alex Welsh's Jazz Band, Hull Jazz Club 2nd. Annual Jazz Band Ball at Goodfellowship, BL's E.C.Jazzmen, Frank Harrison Trio. Actually Alex Welsh didn't turn up due to bad weather. Great night by locals instead.
4/5/78	Stephen Grappelli at New Theatre.
15/3/78	John Barnes, Bruce Turner with Colin Wood Trio at Brunswick Ave. College.
5/12/78	Mike Westbrook Band at Hull Jazz Club, Haworth Arms.
29/6/78	Martin Jones Band, Martin Jones started at George Hotel, MJ's first real band, Ken Ford, Trev Hardy, Bill Cater.
	Blackshaw Band, Colin Chapman, Trevor Hardy (replaced Bob Penwarn) Bill Cater, Alan Blackshaw, Brian Vincent, Joyce Cater, Ken Ford.
	Jazz Diplomats existed around 1960.
	Paragon Jazz Band, forerunner of Blackshaw Band, Dave Tanton (leader) Joyce Rowland, Bill Cater, Alan Blackshaw, Tony Grunhill.

Jazz Venues

There are some vague memories of early jazz at the **Tivoli Tavern**, Mytongate (since demolished) possibly played by a band that included Mike Vyse, though these memories have not been substantiated by any hard evidence. It is thought that the Hull Folk Club used the Tivoli during the Waterson days; there was a large room upstairs that had been used as a boxing gymnasium. Stan Gossip, a well known boxer, was at one time the Landlord.

Circa 1960, SCAT magazine reported that there was a band playing there on Tuesday evenings, it may have been as much a rehearsal band as anything.

The Old Blue Bell in Lowgate was a favourite both with Jazzmen and their audiences. Acoustically, the room was quite good being long and narrow and the seating though cramped was acceptable. Charge for admission varied with the band playing and was 6d. or a shilling (2p or 5p), more expensive when out of town bands were engaged.

Sometimes just an individual musician was booked, the resident bands learnt a lot by playing alongside the 'names' from London. (A personal note - I will not forget splitting a bottle with Sandy Brown, he was staying at the Station Hotel overnight. In those days you could leave a bike in the centre of Hull and not get it nicked!)

The Blue Bell tried to cater for all tastes, certainly they booked a sitar and tabla duo from the West Riding, this must have been around the time of the rise of the Beatles. Eventually the bands transferred to the

Haworth Arms in an attempt to catch the student trade. The Bell was also a Folk Club venue.

The Abercrombie pub was in Campbell Street off Hessle Road and sessions took place in an upstairs room. The music was usually provided by the 2.19 Band and tended to be loud and raw, just what the audience of Art students and similar post-war Bohemians wanted. Not a particularly easy place to get to - two trolley buses for me - how drum kits and basses got there is a bit of a mystery, though some bass players had trailers behind their bikes. The Abercormbie was in operation around about 1956 and the pub was demolished in the '70's along with large chunks of residential streets in the area. A popular venue with that requisite of good jazz places, an 'on' Licence!

This was the place where Bill Cater had to play in his stockinged feet, his compulsive foot-tapping disturbed the bar customers below.

St. Mary's Church Hall, also known as the the Vestry Rooms or **Arlington Hall**, was the original meeting place of the Cottingham Rhythm Society. This was a very popular venue, despite the fact that there was no licence for beer. soft drinks being the order of the day. A very good atmosphere prevailed, helped by the decor, specially created for the jazz sessions. Usually two bands played, the more experienced a set each side of the interval, the interval band maybe the 2 or 3 numbers that they felt most confident with. There was space for dancing and the refreshments included Frank's Famous Franks - hot dogs.

Initially very well supported it became overplayed, the nights it was open being changed to avoid competition with other venues. Transferred to the larger venue of the **Windsor Hall**.

The Windsor Hall was situated in Park Street - at the Anlaby Road end - and it was to here that the Cottingham Rhythm Society transferred. The Cottingham name was dropped and the club became known as the Hull Jazz Club. The Windsor was much larger than the Arlington Hall and the larger capacity was certainly needed as the trad boom continued. Ordinary Club nights attracted large crowds and for 'name' bands it was advisable to buy tickets in advance. There was considerable room for dancing and the decor, novel at the time, consisted of record sleeves from the LP.discs just then coming into fashion. Soft drinks only, although the Argyle pub across Anlaby Road was very close. Most of the big name bands appeared at the Windsor Hall, Bruce Turner, Mick Mulligan with George Melly, Wally Fawkes and Kenny Ball. To name but a few!

The Haworth Arms, Beverley Road, had a large upstairs room capable of seating over 100 people. A popular pub in a residential area and close to the living quarters of a large number of students during the academic year. There were many reasons for the move from the Blue Bell, maybe the most important was the extra capacity of the room. Policy of using local bands was carried on together with the visits from out of town outfits. Run as a club with a moderate fee for membership and reduced prices for members. Attendances suffered a little when the dreaded drink/driving laws began to apply; many gallons of shandy were consumed; Initially the venue was a great success and it was not until 1989 that audiences had dwindled to such an extent as to make the venue uneconomic for trad jazz. Currently presenting a Blues Band which draws a good following.

The Red Cellar was situated in Kingston Square, near the New Theatre, and was the Headquarters of the Young Socialists. As the name implies, it was underground. Not a very large capacity and it had no licence for dancing; as jiving was at that time very much the 'in' thing, this was a handicap. Various bands played there, it seems that the venue did not prove too popular and was closed after a few months. At the time it was in operation the pub venues got the cream of the trad. The Red Cellar opened in February 1960

The Kevin Ballroom, operated by Roy Tilley, housed the Birdland Club. It was situated over the Market Hall and seems to have been mainly a late night venue. Opening in August 1960 according to some reports, other sources indicate that a band was playing jazz there early in 1959, on Tuesday evenings. The late night sessions were often attended by dance band and club musicians after their own jobs had finished for the night, these sessions went on into the early morning.

The **Ship Inn** hosted an unknown band for an unknown length of time.

A Jazz Club opened 'somewhere down De Grey Street' meeting on Wednesdays.

The Grovehill Jazz Club in Beverley (presumably in the **Grovehill Inn**) employed the Geoff Woodhouse Band.

HULL RHYTHM CLUB.

MEMBERSHIP CARD.

N.B.—Members must on all occasions when visiting the Club, carry their Membership Card, which must be produced on demand.

Sub. No. **36.**

RECEIVED OF

Mr. *J Close.*

the sum of **2/6**

being subscription paid

to Hull Rhythm Club.

L. ATACK, *Secretary,*
.. ~~St. Walgrave Street~~, Hull.
Beechwood, 49. Pearson Park

HULL JA~~ZZ~~

Apr.
1954

193

Hull Rhythm Club

There was an enthusiastic attendance at the inaugural meeting of the Hull Rhythm Club, held at their temporary George-st. headquarters on Tuesday. The club, which is designed to foster interest in and the study of real jazz, is open to all—collectors, instrumentalists and fans.

In his opening talk, Mr Alec Mitchell discussed the question of what constitutes good jazz. Gramophone records were played to illustrate various styles of jazz. It is proposed to form a band.

WINDSOR HALL

№ 497

HULL JAZZ CLUB

EILEEN CLOSE
43 HAWTHORN AVE
HULL
1963

Recordings of Hull Jazz and Jazzmen - 1959-62

May 1959	2.19 Jass Band	Folk Song to Jazz Concert, Farmery Hall, Hull.	Recorded by Tony Grunhill on Grundig Tape Recorder with single microphone. Copied to cassettes on request. Unknown number of copies issued. Master tape in possession of Tony Grunhill.
June 1959	2.19 Jass Band	Vestry Rooms, Cottingham. Session of Cottingham Rhythm Society.	as above
July 1959	2.19 Jass band with guest Al Jenner	as above	as above
Sept. 1959	Bob Wallis with 2.19 Jass Band	Blue Bell, Market Place, Hull. Band practice.	as above
May 1960	Drag Kirby's Last Hull.	Windsor Hall, Anlaby Road, Hull. Recording of pick-up group before Drag left Hull to join the Bob Wallis Band.	as above
Feb. 1959	Teddy Barker Quintet.	Students Union, Hull University Concert.	Recorded by Frank Courtney on Ferrograph Tape Recorder & single Resio microphone. Direct cutting acetate discs made by Birkenshaw Recordings of Leeds and privately in Hull. A few are still known to exist. Master tape wiped.
Feb. 1959	Teddy Barker Quintet.	as above	as above

117

Mar. 1960	Teddy Barker Trio	Willerby Manor, Willerby. Recording session.	Recorded by Frank Courtney on Ferrograph with multi-microphone system. Copies of tape provided to Teddy Barker, Tony Gamble, Les Jordon. Master tape wiped.
Mar. 1960	Teddy Barker Trio with Kay Garner (vocals)	as above	as above
Dec. 1960	Teddy Barker Jazz Quintet.	New York Ballroom, Hull. Recording session.	Recorded by Frank Courtney on Ferrograph with multi-microphone system. 50 discs pressed and sold locally on CRS label. A few still exist but are well worn. Master tape wiped.
Jan. 1959	The Jazz Emissaries (Army musicians from band of East Yorks Regiment at Beverley.)	Students Union, Hull University Dance.	Recorded by Frank Courtney on Ferrograph Tape Recorder & single Resio microphone. Direct cutting acetate discs made by Birkenshaw Recordings of Leeds and privately in Hull. A few are still known to exist. Master tape wiped.
Oct. 1959	Bruce Turner Jump Band	Hull Jazz Club, Windsor Hall, Hull. Club session.	Recorded by Frank Courtney on Ferrograph with multi-microphone system. Copied to cassette for friends. Master tape with Frank Courtney.
Jan. 1960	Fairweather-Brown All Stars	Hull Jazz Club, Windsor Hall, Hull. Club session.	Recorded by Frank Courtney on Ferrograph with multi-microphone system. Copied to cassette for friends. Master tape with Frank Courtney.
Oct. 1960	Alex Welsh Jazz Band	as above	as above

April 1961	Geoff Woodhouse Jazz Band	Students Union, Hull University and at Kevin Ballroom, Hull. Recording session for Jazz at Matins LP.	Recorded by Frank Courtney on Ferrograph with multi-microphone system. Some copies to cassettes. Master tape with Geoff Woodhouse. Not known if LP pressed.
Mar. 1962	Geoff Woodhouse Quartet	Club 51, Spring Bank, Hull. Recording session.	Recorded by Frank Courtney on Ferrograph with multi-microphone system. Copied to cassette for friends. Some of Master tape with Frank Courtney.

The Roots

The first Band credited with introducing 'real jazz' to Hull was that of Jack Daniels and his Lions, the time, the middle twenties.

After WW1 the Dance Hall became popular, people needed life and colour and entertainment after the dark days of the war; the disastrous losses of friends and family, the rationing, the Zeppelin raids, had been followed by an influenza epidemic that had cut down thousands of the remaining young and old alike.

The Palais-de-Dance was one of the first, a converted theatre on Anlaby Road, presumably near to the site of the now demolished Palace Theatre. The Jack Daniels Band played there, and a photograph of the line-up of the Band exists with its instruments displayed. Jack Daniels himself played clarinet and piano and his musicians had between them Bass, Baritone, Alto and Soprano Sax. Trumpet, Trombone, Banjo and an elaborate Drum Kit complete with Temple Blocks. Also in the picture are two Mellophones (used for amplifying the clarinet) and a 'singing' megaphone. Eight musicians in the group. Jack Daniels must have been a remarkable character, he was still leading a band in 1980. The Band drew its repertoire from imported American recordings and made transcriptions and arrangements, I suppose into what can only be termed as 'dance jazz'.

The Daniels family as a whole has been very involved with popular music in Hull down the years, everybody who frequented the Dance Halls that sprang up in the twenties and thirties and immediately after the Second World War must have listened and danced to the Maxwell Daniels Band. Maxwell Daniels led on trumpet and was very highly regarded by his fellow musicians. Early on in his career he had won a prime 'Melody Maker' award in open competition and he was a full time professional artist always seeking to improve his own high standards. Mention of his name even now in the nineties brings forth remarks such as "superb tone" and "one of the best around". For many year he ran a music shop on Beverley Road. Just to emphasise his versatility he played trombone with the Society Jazz Band - they put on a series of Thursday lunchtime concerts at the Spring Street Theatre as was. He also played in the orchestra at the new Cecil Cinema, which many people will remember - amazing days to the present generation, they had bands and singers in cinemas!

In spite of the title of this compilation, 'Hull Jazz and Jazzmen', it was obvious before even a start had been made that there would have to be cross references to the Dance Band scene and Clubland. Not even to mention Brass Bands, Folk Bands, Skiffle Groups and Symphonic Orchestras!

Musicians play because they need to play, to most it doesn't matter whether it is the City Hall, a pub, a Club, a Riverboat Shuffle or the back of a float in the Rag Parade; if there is money, no money or beer and a sandwich. Dance Band musicians tell me that they enjoyed playing the same sequence of arranged numbers in strict tempo week after week, that it was never boring, and there was the satisfaction of 'getting it right' one more time. Whatever, the musician must explore the limits of his instrument and in jazz anything goes, the trumpet can squeak, the trombone growl, the singer 'scat'. Relaxation, maybe what they try to do comes off, well, if it doesn't there's always another time!

Maybe the finest example of a Hull musician who played because he had to play was the Hull master trombonist, Harry Chatterton. Harry started in a brass band, playing euphonium 'as a kid' and became one of the greatest jazz trombonists in the country. In demand as a player locally and nationally he appeared with such names as Harold Dawson (before and after the war) Ceres Harper, the Squadronaires, Skyrockets and Peter Yorke (during R.A.F. service) and he also spent two years touring with the Cyril Stapleton Orchestra. During his R.A.F. service he was a member of the R.A.F. Dixieland band which included Ernie Watson of Hull (later lead trumpet with the BBC Northern Dance Orchestra) clarinettist Viv Parker and Ceres Harper, both from Bridlington and a London drummer, George Scott.

After the war he formed a band which played at the Fulford Rooms on Beverley Road seven nights a week and two afternoons!! An 11-piece band playing Stan Kenton and Glen Miller arrangements. The line-up was of two trombones, two trumpets, four sax, accordion, bass and drums. The Fulford Rooms, which had been converted from a house and were run by Mr.F.Hakeney, closed in 1950

In 1951 Harry led a band at the Regal Ballroom, Beverley and this was his venue for seven years. However, the band scene began to alter in the late fifties with the coming of the Groups and Harry took a job at Reckitt's where he worked for 12 years, playing mainly at night and being much in demand for work at the New Theatre.

In 1974, Harry got together a nine-piece band 'The Brass Hats' going the full circle back to his earliest days, but now it was the 'button-down brass approach. Harry was the perfect example of a highly talented man who was prepared to pass on his expertise to young players. He had been coaching brass at the Ambassador Club and was lured along there to be the feature in a 'This is Your Life' evening, well remembered by fellow musicians such as John Canazza, Frank Harrison, Eric Wright and singer Leon Riley.

John Canazza was a bass player of very wide experience. Early on in his career he played piano, he still does for that matter, and had the experience of a Hughie Green 'Opportunity Knocks'. He studied bass at the Royal College of Music, though the professor in charge didn't think much of his instrument - it has five strings, and also played clarinet. He had lots of large dance band experience with Norris Walker who he remembers with great affection. The Walker Band was a very friendly outfit and Norris, always immaculately turned out, got the best jobs at the best venues. For several years the band were resident at the University College Union dance on Saturday evenings.

John was also very much in demand for Club work and wasn't easy to overlook, being six foot five! The club scene was very much in during the late fifties and sixties and live musicians could find plenty of work, but eventually the electronic mechanics produced the one man band and the Disco came in. Must have been nice to be at the Adelaide Club on a Sunday in February 1957 to hear and watch Trevor Hickson, Billy Clutterbrook, Eric Smith on piano, Big John Canazza and Sammy Walsham on drums. Or how about the Majestic Ballroom, Witham, in August 1961, to dance to and be entertained by Harry Chatterton, Gordon Finlay on piano, Don Murray, drums, John Canazza, bass, Gordon Roberts, alto with Leon Riley handling the vocals. Palmy days indeed!

Apart from the 'dance jazz' being played and, no doubt, the Black Bottom and the Charleston being danced to it, there was also a small number of Hull people collecting jazz on record. The number may have been small but there is no doubting the enthusiasm of the collectors, the eight of them listed in the Jazz Collector's Directory in 1948 had amassed between them almost 3000 records. Certainly some of them had been collecting pre-war, the first evidence of a record listening group dates to 1941.

The Hull Rhythm Club of 1942 had several members paying a nominal membership fee of 2/6, the secretary was Mr. L. Atack. Meetings were held presumably in the houses of the members initially, in August 1942 a special meeting was called to discuss the new premises I have taken over by Mr. Atack. These are probably the temporary premises in George Street. The information which had come to light about this era is provided by Mr. Jack Close - he was absent on active service with the Royal Navy for much of the war but maintained his interest in jazz all through those difficult days.

By 1946 the Club was in a position to put on a 'Jam Session' of live music; the first, at the Newington Hall, Albert Avenue, being reported on January 2nd. The musicians were: Ted Barker (pianist) Ted Southern (electric guitar) Alf Joliff (drums) Frank Wade and Jimmy Lucas (who took turns at the bass) Tom Sykes and (no initial given but presumably Billy) Clutterbuck, trumpet, Les Horncastle (clarinet) and Henry Chatterton's powerful trombone was the soul of many choruses. It would be interesting to know just how many of these players had been influenced by wartime contact with the big bands that had been put together by the different sectors of the British and American forces.

Certainly the record listening sessions continued, in October 1950 a small group were to meet to listen to recorded jazz at the premises of a Mr. Hall who was a bootmaker living in Waterhouse Lane. 'Jim' (presumably Jim Stork) was to provide the records. It would be at about this time that the sessions at BALTA House started. The first Riverboat Shuffle was held in August 1953, Coronation Year, and featured the Wool City Jazz Band, the Port of Hull Jazz Band and the

Bob Wallis Jazz Band. The tickets (strictly limited) were 5/- each (25 pence) and another attraction was a river view of the Cleethorpes Illuminations. However, it rained heavily though this did not damp the enthusiasm, sadly the Cleethorpes Illuminations could not be seen.

The membership card of the Hull Jazz Club 1954 was kindly supplied by Mr. Jack Close, he certainly was a very keen enthusiast, he still had retained his membership cards for 100, Oxford Street, 1950, and Humphrey Littleton's Club 1953. Apart from home based jazz he was able to listen to a lot of the American artists as he travelled round the world during his Merchant Navy career. He gives a classic example of the way in which jazz finds and makes friends, having a long correspondence with a Roman Catholic priest that he met in Bermuda. He also just happened to see Louis playing a gig in Buenos Aires!

Ex International Jazz Collectors Directory

(kindly lent by Mr. Jack Close) published by Lawrence Bannister 1948.

John Andrews, Strickland Street, Hull.
400 records of New Orleans, Ory, Lu Watters.

W.A. Cawood, Ventnor Street, Hull.
150 New Orleans, Chicago, Ory, O.D.J.B.

Leo and Ernie Cooper, Bridlington.
460 New Orleans, Bechet.

Tony Grunhill, Princes Avenue, Hull
70 New Orleans, Chicago, Armstrong, Hodges.

Jack Close, Hawthorn Avenue, Hull.
300 Dixieland, Blues. Spanier.

Robert W. Northmore, Holderness Road, Hull.
400 Chicago, New Orleans, McPartland, Wettling.

Donald H. Smith, Hessle, Hull.
Golden Age, Bechet, Beiderbecke, Peppers.

J. Ernest Stork, Priory Rd., Hull.
1,000 New Orleans, Blues, Bechet, Ory

Peter Brian Thompson, Goddard Avenue, Hull.
500 Swing, Be-bop, Goodman, Dixieland.

Where are they now?

Musician	Instrument	Active	Where now?
Eddie Anderson	Washboard,Guitar,Drums	1953	Cottingham
Avo Avison	Trombone	early 50's	London
Denis Aylwin	Bass	1957 -	Gilberdyke
Alan Blackshaw	Bass	1961	Patrington
Geoff Boanas	Trumpet	1953	
Ron Burnett	Trombone	1957	York
'Spiv' Chapman	Trumpet	1960's	Rtd.
Harry Chatterton	Trombone	1930/84	Deceased
'Chez' Chesterman	Trumpet	1957-	London
John Collinson	Banjo/Piano	-	Hastings
Bill Croft	Clarinet	1960's	Newcastle
Bob Curry	Alto		
Eric Dobson	Banjo	1956	Cottingham
Tony Dugdale	Clarinet	1960	United States
Ron Dunn	Drums	1957	United States,Florida
Noel Flint	Bass	1963	Teaching
Graham Galtrey	Clarinet	-	Doncaster
Kay Garner	Vocalist	-	Backing groups, London
Glen Gibb	Trombone	1957	Edinburgh
Mike Gordon	Piano	1957	Scarborough
Tony Grunhill	Drums	1950	Pateley Bridge, Deceased
Mike Heap	Drums	1960	Clubland
Al Jenner	Trumpet	1952	Deceased
Alan Harmer	Piano	1960	Hull
Don Kennington	Tuba	1955	
Brian 'Drag' Kirby	Bass	1956	Deceased
Colin Lilley	Trombone/Bass	1960	Jersey,C.I.
Ted Lewis	Piano	-	Deceased
Bill Newman	Trumpet/Valve Trombone	1957	Surrey
Alan Peacock	Cornet	-	Sutton
Graham Pinkney	Trombone/Vibes	1957	Arranger
Ernie Price	Bass		
Chris Pyne	Trombone	1957	London (Session musician)

Musician	Instrument	Active	Where now?
Mike Pyne	Trumpet/Piano	1957	London (own group)
Alf Rivetts	Tenor	-	Deceased
Gerry Rollinson	Piano	1952	South Africa
Eric Smith	Piano	1950's	
Keith 'Shunt' Smith	Clarinet	1957	Lymne, Cheshire
Cyril Stork	Clarinet	1951	United States
Jim Stork	Alto/Washboard	1951	
Ted Tarling	Clarinet	1957	Local
Dave Thompson	Banjo		
Alan 'Drool' Walker	Trombone	1950's	London
Bob Wallis	Trumpet	1950	Deceased
Roy Wilkin	Drums	1960	Scandinavia
Geof Woodhouse	Clarinet	1957	United States
Mike Vyse	Clarinet	1958	

Currently active jazz musicians in the area.

Dennis AYLWIN	Bass	Dave MITCHELL	Trumpet
Norman BARRON	Trumpet/ Flugelhorn	Dave MILNER	Bass
		Wilf MORAN	Trumpet
Roger CAMERON	Piano	Andy PEACOCK	Trombone
Bill CATER	Trombone	Dave PEACOCK	Banjo
Joyce CATER	Piano	Lenny RANGELEY	Sax
Dave CHALLIS		Pete ROBINSON	Drums
Gordon FINLAY	Piano	Paul ROGERS	
Ken FORD	Banjo/Bass. Promoter	Paul SHARPLES	Trombone
		Martin SHAW	Bass Guitar
Gary GILLYET	Guitar	Paul SHERHERDSON	Drums
Trevor HARDY	Clarinet	Kenny STEVENS	Piano
Albert HARRISON	Bass	Keith STUTT	Drums
Baz HEWLAND	Vibes	Bob SMEATON	Keyboards
Trevor HICKSON	Trumpet	Dave SWANBOROUGH	
John HOLBORN	Clarinet	Terry SWANBOROUGH	Banjo/Bass
Alan HUNTER	Trombone	Eric WRIGHT	Drums
John JACOBSON	Clarinet/Sax	Colin WOOD	Piano
Les JORDAN	Bass		
Martin JONES	Trumpet/ Flugelhorn/ Vocals		

Did you know that?

Derivation of the word Jazz

Alexander's Ragtime Band 1910. Alexander's first name was Charles, abbreviated to Chas. pronounced Chazz, the crown maybe because of inability to pronounce the Ch sound (same trouble with Th, making for Dis and Dat) made it Jazz when demanding an encore. African word Jaiza meaning rumble of distant drums, from 'Dictionary of Word Origins' by J.T. Shipley, published by the Philosophical Library, New York, 1945.

and another:-

Origin southern Negro use, probably since long before 1900. A fast tempo or rhythm frenzy ca.1875. The only original American music traditionally known for its emotional appeal.

Lafardio Hearn (1850 - 1904) found the word in the creole patois of New Orleans. Rhythm based in part on African songs and the work chants of railroad labourers and prisoners. Played almost exclusively in New Orleans particularly in the Storyville District. Bands played on riverboats as far as Minneapolis. Closure of brothels in New Orleans during WW1 caused musicians to go further afield. Jelly Roll Morton started using the word in 1902, as reported by Alan Lomax. Primary meaning given as copulation, from 'Dictionary of American Slang' by H. Wentworth, Ph.D. and Stuart Berg Flexner M.A., published by T.Y.Crowell Co., New York, 1960.

and one from Whitby:-

'Jazzing' is the quick shooting and hauling of nets in the path of the incoming salmon.

Whitby term from 'They Labour Mightily' by Dora M. Walker, published by A. Brown and Co. Ltd., Hull, 1947.

The Training College Jazz Band

The Training College Jazz Band was formed during 1959/1961. 1959 was the first year that male students had been admitted to the College, now part of Humberside Polytechnic and situated on Cottingham Road, adjacent to the University. The line- up consisted of Val Howarth, Piano, Geoffrey Annis and John Windsor, trombones, Arthur Skelton, trumpet, Jed Fewster, clarinet, Ian Lawton, banjo and David 'Spider' Watson on drums. The Band played at College functions, but is not remembered as doing outside work.

Afterword

Thanks to Frank Courtney for the loan of several issues of SCAT; to the Staff of the Local History Library, unfailingly helpful; to the Editor, Hull Daily Mail for permission to reproduce from Jazz Jottings and to everybody that has read this far.

Also to Mr. Jack Close, Mr. Eddie Anderson, Mrs. A. Hakeney, Mr John Carnazza.